BEING OK JUST ISN'T ENOUGH

THE POWER OF SELF-DISCOVERY

DORIS WILD HELMERING

NATIONAL PRESS PUBLICATIONS
A Division of Rockhurst University Continuing Education Center, Inc.
6901 W. 63rd St. • P.O. Box 2949 • Shawnee Mission, Kansas 66201-1349
1-800-258-7246 • 1-913-432-7757

ISBN:1-55852-207-7
Published by National Press Publications
A Division of Rockhurst University Continuing Education Center, Inc.
Printed in the United States of America
18 19 20

Grateful acknowledgment is due the following for permission to reprint previously published material:

Anthony de Mello, S.J. Reprinted with the permission of Doubleday, a division of Bantam Doubleday Dell Publishing Group, Inc. from *The Song of the Bird* by Anthony de Mello, S.J. Copyright 1984 by Anthony de Mello.

Carol Tavris. Reprinted with the permission of Simon & Schuster from *ANGER: THE MISUNDERSTOOD EMOTION* by Carol Tavris. Copyright 1989 by Carol Tavris.

David K. Reynolds. Reprinted with the permission of David K. Reynolds from *Water Bears No Scars*, published by William Morrow and Company, Inc., 1987.

© Gibson Greetings, Inc. Reprinted with permission of Gibson Greetings, Inc., Cincinnati, Ohio 45237. ALL RIGHTS RESERVED.

Ken Keyes. Reprinted with the permission of Ken Keyes. Reprinted from *Handbook to Higher Consciousness* by Ken Keyes, Jr., Fifth Edition, Copyright 1975 by the Living Love Center.

Merle Shain. Reprinted with the permission of Bantam Books, a division of Bantam, Doubleday, Dell Publishing Group, Inc. from *Hearts That We Broke Long Ago* by Merle Shain. Copyright 1983 by Merle Shain.

Moshe Luzzatto. Reprinted with the permission of Feldheim Publishers for the material in *Path of the Just* by Moshe Luzzatto. Copyright © 1966 by Feldheim Publishers.

Oliver Sacks. Reprinted with the permission of Simon & Schuster from *THE MAN WHO MISTOOK HIS WIFE FOR A HAT* by Oliver Sacks. Copyright 1970, 1981, 1983, 1984, 1985 by Oliver Sacks.

Ram Dass and Paul Gorman. Reprinted with the permission of Alfred A. Knopf from *How Can I Help?* by Ram Dass and Paul Gorman. Copyright 1985 by Ram Dass and Paul Gorman.

Sy Miller and Jill Jackson. Reprinted with permission of Sy Miller's daughter, Janet Tache from, *"Let There Be Peace on Earth."* Copyright 1955, 1983.

Thomas Crum, adapted with the permission of Simon & Schuster from *THE MAGIC OF CONFLICT* by Thomas Crum. Copyright 1987 by Thomas Crum.

ADVANCE PRAISE FOR DORIS WILD HELMERING'S BOOK *BEING OK JUST ISN'T ENOUGH*

"Will stimulate you to creatively think about who you really are and what you can imagine yourself to become."

— Mark Victor Hansen, Coauthor — *Chicken Soup for the Soul*

"The next sea change in corporate performance will be improved human relations. This book provides the best platform to begin the discussion."

— J. P. Mulcahy, Chairman, Chief Executive Officer
Eveready Battery Company, Inc.

"Doris speaks to us with a rare combination of compassion and on-target honesty. There is much to gain from reading her remarkable book."

— Wayne W. Dyer, Author — *Your Erroneous Zones*

"Insightful, inspiring, wise and warm, this book takes you on a journey of discovery deep within yourself. Resounding with the richness of real life ... will open your eyes, touch your heart, stir your soul, and change your life and relationships forever. A book to treasure."

— Dianne Hales, Author — *Caring for the Mind*

"A person can use this information to pinpoint his location, identify where he has been, get a handle on where he wants to go and develop a plan for getting there. A road map for the journey of life."

— William Smart, *The Washington Post*

"Wonderful! A truly great book — Sets forth an imaginative way to know how you affect others and they affect you."

— Harold E. Thayer, former Chief Executive Officer
and Chairman of the Board, Mallinckrodt Chemical Co.

"Opens our hearts and minds. Moves us to a new level of insight. A book for each and every one of us!"

— Beth Kubiak Sweeney — Retrouvaille

"Opens windows that many of us keep tightly shut. A winner."

— Worldwide Marriage Encounter

About Rockhurst University Continuing Education Center, Inc.

Rockhurst University Continuing Education Center, Inc., is committed to providing lifelong learning opportunities through the integration of innovative education and training.

National Seminars Group, a division of Rockhurst University Continuing Education Center, Inc., has its finger on the pulse of America's business community. We've trained more than two million people in every imaginable occupation to be more productive and to advance their careers. Along the way, we've learned a few things. Like what it takes to be successful ... how to build the skills to make it happen ... and how to translate learning into results. Millions of people from thousands of companies around the world turn to National Seminars for training solutions.

National Press Publications is our product and publishing division. We offer a complete line of the finest self-study and continuing-learning resources available anywhere. These products present our industry-acclaimed curriculum and training expertise in a concise, action-oriented format you can put to work right away. Packed with real-world strategies and hands-on techniques, these resources are guaranteed to help you meet the career and personal challenges you face every day.

To Skeeter and all people
who believe in integrity,
honesty, hard work, generosity
and kindness.

ACKNOWLEDGMENTS

Writing this book has been a wonderful adventure. In some ways it was like putting a giant puzzle together.

Skeeter, thank you for supporting my idea to go to the mountains for a month and do nothing but write. What a gift that time was. Thanks, too, for your continual support of this project. I often say you're too good to be true. I love you.

Linda Hinrichs, thank you, thank you for the many calls of encouragement while I was writing and for walking me through a few nights of angst when I thought, "What have I gotten myself into!"

To the therapists I work with: Michaeleen Cradock, you are wonderful. I couldn't have left the office in better hands. Pat Cannon, Kathleen Schiffler, and Robyn Cherry, thank you for running the therapy groups and all the extra work you did. Gold stars for everyone.

More gold stars to each of you who graciously let me use your stories in this book. Without them this journey would not have been.

Pat Gregory, you were especially helpful finding books and articles. I think I made at least one difficult request every day for a while, didn't I, Pat? And you never failed to come up with the information. You are a great literary sleuth.

Mary Schwarzbauer and Joan and Joe Hoffman, thank you for additional sleuthing.

Bill Hendricks of National Seminars Group, you're one super smart human being. Thanks for encouraging me to add more business examples to the text and for immediately recognizing what this book is really all about.

Judy Cassidy, Linda Hinrichs, and Bethe Growe — many kudos for the time you gave reading and rereading the manuscript. It would not have been so clear without your wise input.

It's often tough to give a book a title, and many people contributed ideas. The funniest suggestion for a title came from Dave Gosnell. He wanted to call the book *You: The Whole Enchilada*. Others who offered numerous suggestions included Richard Rennecamp, Ava Ehrlich, Sheldon Korklan and Carolyn and John Dyess. Gary Truitt, nice job! Gary came up with the actual title, but all of you should take a bow.

I also thank Beth Lieberman; April Winkelmann; Machelle Hines; Jo Oberreither; Kathy Meder; Martha Scharff; Doris Drewry; Anita Devon; Julie Belt; John Robinson; Diane Ray; Sheri Cox; John, Paul, and Anna-Mary Helmering; and Mom and Dad. Your suggestions and unending support made it possible for this book to happen.

What a wonderful, terrific, great crew!

Legend Symbol Guide

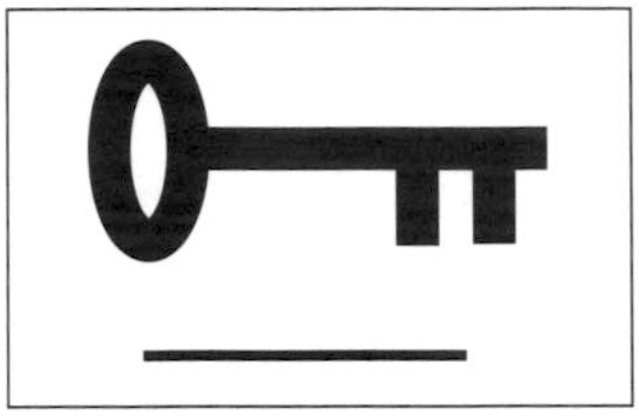

Key issues to learn and understand for future application.

?

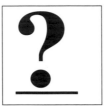

Questions that will help you apply the critical points to your situation.

✓

Checklist that will help you identify important issues for future application.

CASE STUDY

Real-world case studies that will help you apply the information you've learned.

CONTENTS

CHAPTER 1

Why Go Through Life and Not Understand Yourself?

> ***"Here is the test to find whether your mission on earth is finished: If you're alive, it isn't."***
>
> Richard Bach

A story is told of a man and wife who would sit and meditate each morning before allowing the day's events to take over their lives. Every day as they were meditating, they would hear the impatient honking of a horn next door, signaling the arrival of the neighbor's carpool.

One morning after meditating, the man said to his wife, "If I had the power, I would will that all four tires of that honking car would go flat every day as he got in his car."

The wife replied, "My, my. That's rather drastic."

After thinking it over, the man said, "If I had the power, I would will that the horn on that fellow's car would never work and could never be fixed."

The wife's response: "That's still a bit drastic."

Some hours later the man came back with a slight smile and said, "If I had the power, I would will that the horn wouldn't work, but only in front of our neighbor's house."

The wife said, "That's better."

That night, as the couple got into bed, the man said, "If I had the power, I would be so intently involved in my meditating that I wouldn't even hear the horn."[1]

What I love about this story is the man's willingness to continue to search for the best response. In order to feel less frustrated and more in control of his life, the man went through a series of responses. He went from thinking vindictive thoughts and "Why can't the other guy change" to focusing on himself and what he could do differently.

• • •

Paul, our son, had just graduated from college, was living away from home and announced that he was going to get a dog. On hearing his news, I immediately said, "That's ridiculous. You're in between jobs. You don't know where you're going to live. And if you come home and live with us for a while, you'll want to bring the dog with you, and we don't want another dog."

I ended my speech with, "You're just not thinking."

Frustrated, Paul said, "Mom, you don't understand. I'm grown up. I can take care of a dog. Why can't you be supportive?"

In my blindness I shot back, "I am being supportive. I'm thinking of the consequences of what a dog means."

Again he said, "You're being critical, Mom. You're not being supportive."

Indeed, he was right. I was being critical. I chose to focus on the negative aspects of owning a dog. I also was trying to convince him to live his life the way I thought he should live it. I was not respectful of his decision, nor was I being supportive.

What I could have done when Paul told me he was getting a dog was to be quiet. I could have listened. If and when he needed to move back home, I might have said, "We'll take you, but not the dog." Or, "You can live with us, but the dog has to stay outside." Because of my son's confrontation that day, I had a new understanding of myself, painful as it was.

> ***"Man cannot discover new oceans unless he has courage to lose sight of the shore."***
>
> God's Little Instruction Book

• • •

I find that most people have a minimal awareness of themselves — how they behave, the thoughts and feelings that drive their behavior, the effects their actions have on others, and ultimately the misery their behavior creates in their own lives.

Most of us live our entire life without truly understanding ourselves. We may realize that sometimes we talk too much, advise too quickly, get too angry or fail to do what we have promised. On a thoughtful, introspective day, we may admit to ourselves that sometimes we feel smug over a friend's plight or

> ***"What lies before us and what lies behind us are small matters compared to what lies within us."***
>
> Henry David Thoreau

that we value looks and money over integrity and kindness. But we rarely allow ourselves to go much beyond these realizations.

If a crisis comes along — a mate leaves, we lose a job, we can't seem to get along with a fellow worker, a child strays too far from the path we expected her to follow — we may take the time to look more closely at ourselves and even change some of our behaviors. Once the crisis is past, however, we become lazy. Or we get so caught up in the process of living that we fail to continue to explore who we are and how our actions affect every relationship we have.

One author wisely tells us, ***"A life not examined is like an unopened letter."***[2] And centuries ago Plato wrote, ***"The unexamined life is not worth living."***[3]

If you think about it, coming to an understanding of yourself — why you obsess on certain thoughts, why you feel a particular way when someone else in the same situation feels an entirely different way, why you behave as you do — should be one of your most important tasks in life. Yet few take up the challenge.

I invite you to take up the challenge and come with me on an introspective journey where you will come to know yourself as never before. Or as St. Paul says, ***"Wake up, sleeper, rise from the dead ... "***[4] It's time to understand yourself.

2

CHAPTER 2

Are You an Outer-Focused or Inner-Focused Person?

People tend to focus their attention either outward on others or inward on themselves. And because they focus their attention differently, they think and behave differently.

Recently, I was at a board meeting where a number of us were sitting around the table talking, drinking coffee and waiting patiently for the meeting to start when another member walked in. He greeted us good-naturedly, took his place at the table, and then said, "Can't a guy get a cup of coffee around here?"

I think this man had no realization of how his comment invited someone else to take care of him, to wait on him. Sure enough, another board member got up, went over to the credenza, asked the fellow what he took in his coffee and fixed it for him. The man who covertly asked to be waited on is inner-directed. His focus of attention is himself. The woman who got the coffee is outer-directed. Her focus of attention is other people.

"Each relationship nurtures a strength or weakness within you."

Mike Murdock

"Some people say they haven't yet found themselves. But the self is not something one finds; it is something one creates."

Thomas Szasz

Your Focus Determines Your Behavior

Now I'm going to describe three people who have very different ways of thinking and consequently behaving. Chances are, you're like one of these people.

CASE STUDY

First, there's Maggie. Her thinking and behavior are mainly focused on others. Next, you'll meet Bill, who is mainly focused on himself. And then there's Al, who seems to be oblivious of others and only partially aware of himself. As you read, ask yourself: ***Am I like this person? And if so, how?***

Meet Maggie

Maggie's 36, has two children and is a computer scientist. When Maggie wakes up in the morning, the first thing she thinks about is the children's schedule. When she remembers that Pete's soccer game is at 5:30, she immediately thinks how she's going to juggle her time so she can leave work early. When she hears on the radio that the temperature is dropping, she calls to her daughter to take a jacket. She goes outside to cut some roses for the office before the cold weather finishes them off.

As Maggie fixes coffee, she telephones her mother to remind her of Pete's game. She gives the cat fresh water and adds food to his bowl. She pours herself coffee, calls to Pete to hurry and reminds him not to forget his soccer shoes.

When she gets to the office, she tells the receptionist that she likes her blouse. She is very free with compliments, and sometimes criticisms. She gives a fellow engineer an article she cut out for him the night before. She works at her terminal with few breaks. If someone has a technical problem, Maggie is the person who can be depended on to take the time to figure out a solution. If people seem unhappy in her department, she brings them little presents. Sometimes Maggie gets so tired and stressed with everything she takes on, she can be found in the washroom crying.

Are you like Maggie? Do you know anyone else who thinks and acts like her?

> ***"The greatest enemy of your creative powers is smug complacency."***
>
> Nido R. Qubein

Meet Bill

Bill's 47, married, has two teenagers and is an attorney.

As soon as the alarm sounds, Bill's out of bed. He throws on his running clothes, does a few warm-up exercises and flies out the door. By the time he gets back from running, the family is up. When Bill notices that his wife is about to take her shower, he gives her a sheepish grin and says, "You don't mind if I go first, do you, honey?"

After his shower, he fixes himself cereal and asks his son what's happening. As his son talks, Bill reads the newspaper. When he's finished his cereal, he jumps up, grabs his briefcase and says flirtatiously, "Doesn't anyone have a kiss for me?" His family gives him kisses and he's off.

When Bill gets to work, he meets with one client after another. Because he overschedules himself, he often runs late. When he makes a promise to do something, he frequently forgets. If he gets confronted about not doing something, he becomes annoyed and thinks the other person has no right telling him what to do. He starts a conversation in the middle of what he's thinking, and people are always playing catch-up, trying to figure out what he's talking about. Those in his firm see him as bright, funny and a go-getter. But on any day of the week, there is someone who is annoyed with him. He has a hard time understanding why.

Recently Bill telephoned me (we talk every couple of weeks), and when I answered the phone, he said, "I've been trying to reach you for an hour. Where have you been?" I shook my head and smiled. I do love Bill, but he sure operates as though he's the center of the world.

Are you like Bill? Who else do you know who acts like him?

CASE STUDY

Meet Al

Al's married, has three children and is an insurance adjuster. Al is getting ready for work. The television is reporting the events of last night. Al only halfway listens. When his wife asks if he's going to be able to make their youngest son's soccer game, he says he's not sure. He gives no further thought to her question.

When his daughter rushes in to ask if he can pick her up from swim practice, he says, "Probably."

When she insists, "Daddy, I've got to know — I have to make plans," he responds, "I guess I can."

As he pours himself coffee, he asks, "Has anyone seen the milk?" His wife says, "It's here on the table."

He eats his breakfast quietly and halfway listens as his wife checks schedules. When she leans down to kiss him goodbye,

"Every man I meet is in some way my superior; and in that I can learn from him."

Apples of Gold

he turns his cheek so she can kiss him. When she says, "Say, what do you think of my new dress?" he notices it for the first time, smiles and says, "It's nice."

Al's a hard worker. Most people at his company like him and think he's a nice guy, but nobody knows him very well because he doesn't talk much. Even in a brainstorming session that involves his department, he rarely makes a comment. He doesn't get angry. He's not critical or sarcastic. He's not rude. He simply goes along with whatever.

Are you similar to Al? Do you work with anyone like him or have friends who resemble him?

Differences Between an Outer-Focused and Inner-Focused Person

Here are some interesting differences that social scientists have observed about inner-focused and outer-focused people. Read the list with yourself in mind.

- An outer-focused person feels love when giving; an inner-focused person feels love when receiving.

- An outer-focused feels powerful when she does things for others; an inner-focused feels powerful when he gets others to do things for him.

- An outer-focused is very concerned with the opinions of others; an inner-focused doesn't concern himself too much with what others think.

- An outer-focused lectures, gives advice, corrects, analyzes and forever wants to change people; an inner-focused doesn't want to change, nor does he have a need to change others.

- An outer-focused usually leans forward when she talks; an inner-focused leans slightly backward when he talks.

- An outer-focused gives energy, an inner-focused takes energy.

- An outer-focused wants togetherness; an inner-focused wants to be left alone.

- An outer-focused pursues people; an inner-focused allows himself to be pursued.

Notice I used "she" when describing an outer-focused person and "he" when describing an inner-focused. This is because in my clinical experience, most women focus their attention outward on others, and most men focus their attention inward on themselves. This doesn't mean that some women aren't inner-focused and some men outer-focused. Nor does it mean that an outer-focused woman never thinks of herself or that an inner-focused man never considers others.

On first reading, some people also get the idea that an inner-focused person is shy and quiet, whereas an outer-focused person is outgoing and talkative. This may or may not be so. An outer-focused individual may be very shy and an inner-focused may be talkative. An outer-focused may be low-energy and an inner-focused, high-energy.

"Nothing is all wrong. Even a clock that has stopped running is right twice a day."

Anonymous

Incidentally, have you ever wondered how someone could be watching a good movie on television and, right in the middle of it, decide to get up and go to bed? Well, if you're an inner-focused person, it's easy because you don't get caught up in what's happening on television. You realize you're tired, and you go to bed. If you're an outer-focused individual, no matter how tired you are, you have to see the ending.

This same principle applies to the way people use their television remote control. An inner-focused person will continually flip channels because it's hard to hold his attention. Even if he's watching television with other people, he'll pick up the remote and change channels. He focuses on what interests him, and he forgets other people are watching. An outer-focused person rarely changes channels because she gets involved in whatever she's watching.

The differences between outer- and inner-focused also account for the reason why women generally know what gifts others would enjoy. They are used to thinking about others and what they like in life.

Is Your Focus Genetic?

Many social scientists believe that your focus has a biological basis and that you come into this world with a predisposition to be either outer- or inner-focused. Then a variety of other factors come into play which determine how strongly outer- or inner-focused you are. These factors include your sex, birth order, your parents' expectations and everyday behavior that was modeled for you.

In addition to these influences, society plays a large part in the way you think, feel and behave. Because males get more attention than females (some studies say two to three times as much), men come to expect to be the center of attention. It's what they have always known. Because little girls see little boys getting more attention, they fall into step and give attention.

Sometimes an unexpected event will serve to modify a person's focus. For example, an inner-focused man who loses his job may come to look more outside himself and be more sympathetic to others who have had financial reversals. An inner-focused man may become more outer-focused, more conscious of his family, if he experiences a major illness. On the other hand, an outer-focused woman may become more inner-focused if she has a problem at work, or if she herself falls ill.

> ***"Our problem with change is not our inability, but our resistance."***
>
> Al Schneider

Perhaps we adjust our focus during a time of crisis, with an inner-focused person turning outward and an outer-focused person turning inward, as our usual way of thinking and behaving seems to have failed us.

Many women have told me that when they were in their twenties and thirties, they were too outer-focused, often worrying about others to the exclusion of themselves. By their mid-forties they started to focus more on themselves and what they wanted in life.

Conversely, many men often start out being extremely inner-focused, and by their mid-forties, they become more focused on others. Through time and experience, most people adjust and modify their focus. But your basic center of attention does not change.

> ***"Do or do not. There is no try."***
>
> Yoda

This was pointed out to me most poignantly some years ago. My friend Betty was dying of cancer. It was a Wednesday evening, and I had the strongest urge to see her. When I walked into her bedroom, she said, "Doris, I'm dying."

I said, "I know, Betty. What can I do?"

She looked at me and said, "Will you please clean my bedroom and bathroom? I know that must sound silly, but please will you?"

I said, "I understand." I got busy and dusted her dresser, folded her robe and straightened some magazines and papers. I went in her bathroom and cleaned the sink and mirror and emptied the wastebasket.

When I walked back into Betty's bedroom, I asked if there was anything else I could do. By this time her daughter had come into the room. She asked if her daughter would put "Madame Butterfly" on the stereo. The three of us sat silently, listening to the aria. Betty looked at us, smiled and said, "Now I'm fine."

Several hours later she died.

What Betty needed first was to have her outside world in order. Once this happened, she was able to relax and turn inward.

Too Much Attention Focused on Others

Many people, particularly women, think that being outer-focused is better, more admirable and virtuous. Certainly it is a better world when people look out for each other and are generous, giving and responsive to others' needs. But sometimes outer-focused people go overboard, and their giving becomes smothering and detrimental.

• • •

CASE STUDY

I'm seeing a woman in therapy who is too centered on her son. If he's happy and things are going well for him in school and with his friends, she's happy. If her son does poorly on a test, has a run-in with a teacher or is snubbed by another child, she takes his side and goes into action. She does too much to ease his pain. She might call the teacher and plead her son's case. She will take him to a movie, plan an overnight with some of his friends, run him to the music store to pick out a few CDs or go to the library and help him with a paper. This child is not learning how to take responsibility for himself. He's not learning how to handle problems and disappointments. He's not building his own resources, which he will need. This woman's happiness is too dependent on her son's happiness.

The following story has great implications for those who are too outer-focused:

A monkey was sitting in a tree looking at the water below. All of a sudden, the monkey hopped down, grabbed a beautiful salmon from the water and placed it on a high tree branch.

The monkey's friend looked at her and said, "What on earth are you doing with that salmon?"

"I am saving it from drowning," the monkey happily replied.[5]

Are you like this monkey?

Too Much Attention Focused on Yourself

If you're assertive and too inner-focused, you are likely to behave as though you're the only person whose wants and feelings count. This behavior not only causes others pain but in the end causes you pain.

Several days after I had given a talk on this subject, the president of a large corporation telephoned and introduced himself. He said, "I recognize myself. I'm one of those types who's been accused of always doing what I damn well please. What's the cure?"

I half-laughed and said, "You have two assignments. These assignments are easy for some people and difficult for others. For you, they will be difficult."

He said, "I can handle it."

I said, "Okay. The first thing you do — every time you make a decision to do something, be aware of how your decision is going to impact or affect another person. If the other person is going to be adversely affected, consider an alternative plan."

"Be a lamp in the chamber if you can't be a star in the sky."

Apples of Gold

"The second thing — keep all promises. If you promise to telephone someone on Monday, do it. If you promise to be home by six, be home by six. No excuses."

I've never heard from the man again. And I've often wondered if he was able to keep his assignment.

If this were your assignment, would you have difficulty doing it?

> ***"Patience — in time the grass becomes milk."***
>
> Apples of Gold

If you're inner-focused and your tendency is to be passive, you also don't take others into account. Your style of behaving is plodding along and doing your thing — not sharing yourself or your ideas, not planning, not making decisions. As a result, others become responsible for the thinking, planning and decision-making. Another tragedy is that you miss out on being an integral part of someone else's life and having others be a part of yours.

I saw a man in therapy who fits this description. Ed came to see me because his wife was threatening to leave him. He never talked. I put him in a therapy group where he learned to interact with others. One of his goals was to reveal something about himself each week. A second goal was to have a conversation with someone and learn something about their life. A third goal was to give his wife three compliments a day. For one year Ed kept a written record.

The night he graduated from his group, he said, "I thank you. My wife thanks you. My children thank you." I will never forget how pleased he was. I gave him a pat on the back and knew that his thank-you's were about becoming an introspective, sharing, giving human being.

A New Direction

Although your inclination to focus outward on others or inward on yourself isn't going to change, you can become more balanced. This means focusing inward on yourself and asking what is best for you, as well as focusing outward on others and asking what would be best for them. If you and the other person can't be satisfied at the same time, compromise. Take turns giving and getting. Not too much giving, not too much taking. Once you have mastered a balanced focus, all your actions will imply, "I count and you count."

Ask yourself: ***Do my thinking and actions imply an "I count, you count" philosophy?***

Is my focus in life a balanced one?

CHAPTER 3

Are You Aware of Your Psychological Boundary Lines?

Recently I was having dinner at a restaurant with a few friends and decided to order dessert. When my dessert came, one of my friends said, "Oh, let me taste." She then reached over with her fork and took a bite. Although I said, "Sure, fine," I didn't like that she had stuck her fork in my food. I'm very territorial. Of course, someone taking an unexpected bite of my dessert is not going to ruin a friendship, but there are psychological boundaries that get crossed each day at home and at the office that do create tension and bad feelings.

> ***"Everybody is one of a kind."***
> Dr. George Crane

You're Invading My Space

As a newborn, you don't recognize any margins or boundaries between yourself and the world. You do not distinguish between your hands, the bars of your crib and your mother's body. The merging between yourself and others is seamless. By the time you're six months old, you have a basic awareness of your hand versus your mother's hand. You are beginning to understand your separateness.

> ***"To break a habit, create another one that will erase it."***
> Al Schneider

By age two, a sense of self starts to emerge. You look into the mirror and you recognize yourself. You are becoming aware of your own abilities. As you climb the stairs, you say, "Go up." You start to realize that you have some power to influence others. You look at your mother and say, "Sit."

As your sense of self grows, your sense of possession — what is yours, and what is yours to control — is also growing. By age three, you are starting to define your psychological boundaries. If another youngster comes along and plops down next to you, you may start pushing and shoving him away. By your actions you're saying, "My space, my territory. Move over, Buster." You not only define your territory, you protect it, much like a country that protects its borders.

As you move into grade school, you continue to define your psychological boundaries. Because these boundaries are largely a matter of interpretation, your rights versus another person's rights, you are most influenced by the people around you, mainly family. For example, in some families, people drink out of each other's glasses and use each other's hairbrushes and bath towels without a thought. In other families the members are more territorial: "That's my chair." "I told you I don't want you using my washcloth." "Get out of my purse." "Do not go in my toolbox." "Stay out of my drawers."

As an adult, you may follow these childhood directives, adjust or change them. This changeability is dependent on two things: your relationship with the person who has crossed the invisible line you've drawn and your own level of acceptance that day.

For example, you may start out not using anyone else's hairbrush and not allowing anyone to use yours. Then one day you can't find your brush, and your good friend says, "Here. Use mine." You may feel somewhat uncomfortable, but you use her brush. If this happens a few more times, you may come to the point of using her brush without experiencing any negative thoughts or bad feelings. In essence, you have erased this psychological boundary. Certainly your boundary lines are less rigid with family than with friends and less rigid with friends than with co-workers. If your wife or best friend reads one of your letters without asking, it might not bother you. If you catch an acquaintance doing the same thing, it may be a whole different story.

Your mood, how you think and feel on a particular day, also affects your response. Some days your acceptance level is high; other days it's low. If you and your friend are having a pleasant day, it's no problem when she helps herself to some food in your refrigerator. If you're aggravated with her, or you're having a bad day for some other reason, your response to her invasion of your refrigerator may be negative.

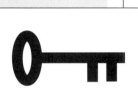

You might not mind your daughter going into your closet and rummaging around for something to wear. You might even be pleased that the two of you share clothes. However, if you're annoyed at her for leaving a messy kitchen, another area you interpret as your domain, you may immediately draw an invisible line around the rest of your things. Now if she walks into your closet, you may say in an irritated voice, "Get out of my closet. Those are my clothes."

Your daughter may think of you as someone who can't make up her mind. One day it's fine that she goes through your clothes. The next day you're all hot and bothered. What neither of you understands is that people are always readjusting their psychological boundary lines.

A Quiz: Discovering Your Boundary Lines

In order to discover some of your psychological boundaries, take a moment and answer the following 10 questions. There are no right or wrong answers. Your answers, however, may surprise you, and most certainly they will give you important information about yourself and your relationships.

1. Do you have a problem with someone going into your desk drawer to get a pair of scissors or a stapler?

   ____

   ____

2. Does it bother you if your mate opens your mail or someone at your office reads your faxes?

   ____

   ____

3. Are you annoyed if a friend comes to your home and turns on the television or stereo without asking?

   ____

   ____

4. Would you have a problem if someone wrote in the margin of one of your books?

5. Have you ever been irritated with a friend for forming a friendship with someone who was initially your friend?

6. Would you feel annoyed if someone stood over your shoulder and watched what you were writing on your PC or picked up a folder on your desk and flipped through it?

7. Would you have negative feelings if you left your sweatshirt at a friend's home and when she returned it, she said she'd worn it the previous night?

8. If a friend comes for a visit, do you have a problem with him going into your refrigerator to get something to eat? How about if he goes into your cabinet, gets a glass and pours himself a soda?

9. When paying bills, working or reading, do you prefer quiet?

10. Would it bother you if a co-worker used your idea at a meeting without acknowledging that the idea was yours?

Here's how I, myself, would answer the first five questions. As you read over my answers, compare them to yours.

1. I have no problem with someone going into my desk drawer for a pair of scissors. I would feel slightly annoyed if they ate all my cookies, which I also keep in my desk. Helping themselves to a few would be fine.

2. I would be bothered if my husband opened my mail without asking. When I'm away on a trip and he asks if he should open it, I say yes, but I feel a twinge of uncertainty, a little intruded upon. Reading my fax? I don't like it when people read my faxes, especially before I get a chance to read them.

3. If a friend came to my home and turned on the television or stereo without asking, I'd be annoyed. If she asked if she could turn it on, no problem.

4. If a person wrote in my book in pencil — my sense of nosiness, wanting to see what he had written, would override my annoyance. If the person wrote in pen, I definitely would feel a boundary had been crossed.

5. I have felt somewhat unsettled when a good friend of mine has befriended another friend, and I've been left out in some way. I don't like that I feel this way, but I do.

As you can see, my answers reveal that I'm fairly territorial. I don't like people invading what I define as my friends, my possessions. You, on the other hand, may be more fluid, less possessive.

> ***"Change your thoughts and you change your world."***
>
> William James

Why Understanding Boundaries Is Important

> ***"We first make our habits, and then our habits make us."***
>
> Charles Noble

Because your psychological boundaries are invisible, chances are you don't even know they exist until someone crosses one of them. But when a person steps over the line, your response will be a negative thought, such as "Hey you, what's the deal!" This thought will be followed by a rush of adrenalin, culminating in feelings of anxiousness or annoyance. This entire response takes less than a second.

In therapy I continually see people who are unaware of their own or another's boundaries. More often than not, this lack of awareness leads to trouble.

A boundary that is definitely one to be aware of is your psychological noise boundary. How much noise and how much silence are you comfortable with?

If a husband enjoys quiet and his wife likes to talk, her talking may make him uneasy. On some level he feels as though he's being invaded. He may address his discomfort by walking out of the room or tuning his wife out.

The wife, on the other hand, may feel anxious when her husband doesn't talk. One might say her psychological noise boundary has been invaded by his silence. She may address her uneasiness by chasing after him to talk or by picking a fight to get him talking.

Here's another example. One spouse likes the television on and the volume high. The other prefers the television off, but if it's on, she prefers the volume low. When the volume is up, she feels intruded on; when it's down, he's uncomfortable.

One couple I worked with had trouble when the husband watched sporting events on television, particularly football. His wife said she could not bear the continual talking of the announcer and the constant roar of the crowd. It made her so anxious that she felt like going over to the television and clicking it off or running out of the house, both of which she actually had done. Once she was aware of her noise boundary and was able to talk about it, her agitation lessened when her husband watched football. He, on the other hand, has attempted to keep the volume turned down in deference to his wife.

Another psychological boundary involves information — what information is okay to share and with whom. The husband may see no problem in telling his best friend that he and his wife have been trying to have a baby, while the wife may think revealing this information is a betrayal of her and the marriage. On the other hand, this wife feels it's perfectly acceptable to tell her parents her husband's income, whereas the husband thinks it's nobody's business but his and his wife's.

This same information boundary can be crossed at the office. You're at a meeting and you casually share some findings with another company. Your partner becomes perturbed and thinks you've divulged too much information. You interpret his response as being ridiculous and a little paranoid, while he thinks you're a blabbermouth.

> ***"Friends are made by many acts — and lost by only one."***
>
> Apples of Gold

Somtimes a person will feel her boundary line has been crossed if a friend dresses in a similar manner, chooses the same hairstyle, buys an identical automobile or starts wearing the same perfume. When you have a thought such as "Stop copying me" or "Stop trying to act like me," it indicates that you are feeling invaded. In other words, a psychological boundary has been crossed.

Another boundary people rarely talk about but which causes a good deal of emotional pain is the boundary line of friendship. For example, Sally introduces Ron to Sherry. Next, Ron and Sherry are getting together without her, and Sally is feeling not only odd-person-out but that a line has been crossed.

Friends, information, noise, space, things and places — are all subject to invisible lines of demarcation.

A Thinking Exercise

Now that you have become aware of a number of your psychological boundaries, think about one of them — for example, someone going into your desk drawer — and answer the following questions.

1. When I feel intruded upon, what do I say to myself that causes me to feel a negative response?

2. Is my reaction linked to my childhood? Does it have anything to do with what my parents did or said?

3. Would my best friend or my mate feel the same if this happened to him or her?

4. Is this an issue I want to address with the person who I think crossed the line? If so, what will I say to get my point across without offending him or her?

Think of another boundary line you've discovered, and run through the questions again. Learning to think in this way keeps misunderstandings, arguments and bad feelings over these issues to a minimum.

No Rights or Wrongs, 'Tis Thinking That Makes It So

Remember, there are no rights or wrongs when it comes to psychological boundaries. What you define as right is a matter of how you think, how you interpret a particular event. Psychological boundaries are also subject to change, depending on how you feel on a particular day and your relationship with the person who stepped over the line.

Although Shakespeare's Hamlet was talking about an entirely different matter, he just as easily could have been talking about psychological boundaries when he said, ***"for there is nothing either good or bad, but thinking makes it so."***[6]

CHAPTER 4

Do You Know and Practice the Eight Principles of Love?

"One kind word can warm three winter months."

Japanese proverb

CASE STUDY

Dick came to see me because his wife was going to leave him. It was our first therapy session, and he was in great emotional pain.

One of the first things I asked Dick was if he knew why his wife wanted to leave him. He said he wasn't sure.

I asked what his wife had complained about through the years. He said his wife thought he always had to have everything his way.

"Is this true?" I asked.

He said, "Not always."

He related that when he was a child, his father was in charge of the decision-making. He guessed he had some of those same tendencies.

I asked if he could think of any specific incidents when he insisted on his way.

He said his wife wanted to put an addition on their house with money she had inherited from her grandmother, but he had nixed the idea. He said that at one time she wanted to go back to school and finish her education. He was against it, so she never went back. In retrospect he's sorry that he didn't encourage her.

"Have you ever told your wife that you've regretted taking that stance?" I asked.

"No," he said, "I've never brought it up. My philosophy is to let sleeping dogs lie."

4

C A S E S T U D Y

I said, "Sometimes they're not sleeping." He smiled in recognition.

I asked Dick what other complaints his wife had. He said she thought he had a bad temper.

"What do you say?" I asked.

"Sometimes I do," he admitted.

I questioned whether he had ever hit his wife when he was angry. "Never," he said indignantly. "I would never touch her."

"How about name-calling or intimidating looks?"

"Sometimes," he admitted.

I asked if he was a pouter. He looked at me and said, "How did you know?" I said that often when a person thinks he should be in charge, he uses a variety of behaviors to get his way. Pouting is one of them.

Dick said, "My wife's sarcastic. And she's very critical."

My response, "That doesn't make you want to be with her, does it, Dick?" I could see the wheels turning.

"So how long can you pout, Dick — a couple of days?" I asked.

"I've been known not to talk for a while," he said.

I pushed. "What's a while, Dick?" He grinned at having been caught. "A couple of days, maybe a week," he said.

I asked what other reasons his wife might have for leaving him.

"Golf," he said. "She thinks I like golf better than I like her."

"Do you?" I asked.

He laughed and said, "No."

"How much do you play?" I inquired.

He grinned and said, "Every chance I get. I love the game."

He offered that maybe his wife was mad because he forgot her birthday. She had given him a surprise party for his birthday, and then he forgot hers. "But, honest," he said, "it wasn't intentional."

When I asked what he'd done to make up for forgetting her birthday, he said he thought he had apologized. And he sent her flowers, which she promptly threw in the trash.

I kept pushing. "Anything else your wife complains about?"

"She's always saying I don't love her."

"If you did love her, what would you be doing differently?" I questioned.

> ***"Isn't it a pity, forgetting to give back."***
>
> George Harrison

"I guess I'd listen more. Maybe spend more time doing what she wanted. Tell her I love her. That's a big one. I'm not a bad guy, you know. I just don't think about those things."

"So why not, Dick? I bet your wife has told you plenty of times," I countered.

"You're right," he said, "she's told me plenty."

Unhappily for Dick and his wife, Dick does not know how to love.

• • •

Many people think they know how to love because they have allowed themselves to fall in love, perhaps many times. Or they think of their children or a special friend and feel an overwhelming sense of closeness. Actually these feelings, traditionally spoken of as love, are really feelings of intimacy, which I address in a later chapter.

Love is dynamic, powerful and active. Love is an action verb — something one human being does for another. And not necessarily because he feels close or connected with the other person but because he believes the other person has value and worth.

> ***"There are some days when I think I'm going to die from an overdose of satisfaction."***
>
> Salvadore Dali

What is love? Love is listening. Love is remembering. Love is giving, receiving, respecting, confronting and disciplining. Love is playing. Love is forgiving. After you read the following stories, perhaps you will be able to better answer the question: ***Do you know how to love?***

1. Love Is Listening

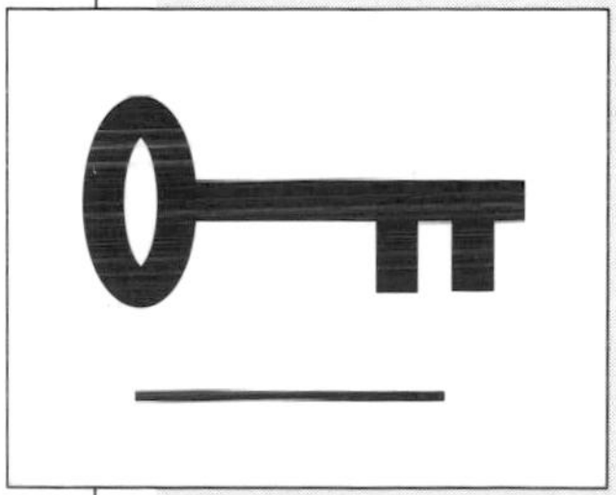

If you know how to love, you listen.

When someone talks, you hear. Your purpose is to discover something new. You do not rush to judge, or problem solve, or analyze, or lecture. You listen with your face, your eyes, your mouth, your whole body. You don't wait for a chance to break in and tell your story. You focus on what the other person is saying. You ask thoughtful questions that are in keeping with the topic. You say, "uh huh," nod, smile, laugh and try to put yourself in the other person's shoes. You do not glaze over, make a to-do list in your head or mentally take a trip to Bermuda. You travel along with the person talking.

As I was writing this book, my friend Linda called every so often to find out how it was going. She would say, "Want to read me a few pages?" And sometimes I did.

As she listened, she'd interject, "Yes ... yes ... good ... right on."

Whenever I telephone Linda, she's enthusiastic. She knows how to make me feel special. She's a true friend to people. She gives time, attention and compliments. If you're in trouble and call Linda, she doesn't put you on hold. She listens. Linda knows how to love.

> ***"Take away love and our earth is a tomb."***
>
> Robert Browning

• • •

A woman was telling her husband about having dinner with their oldest son and how grown up he seemed. As she was talking, her husband interrupted and said, "Did you tell him to wear sunscreen?"

She said, "Sunscreen? What are you talking about?"

The husband said he had just seen a show on television about skin cancer and how everyone who's out in the sun should wear sunscreen. Needless to say, this man had not been listening to his wife.

Perhaps it's because we have so many places to go, things to do and people to see that we've lost the art of listening, the art of hearing. It's always a treat for me to watch someone listen and not interrupt. When you listen and hear, you give the gift of self-esteem. You make the other person feel important and loved.

Do you listen to others?

2. Love Is Remembering

If you know how to love, you remember. If your friend has a job interview or a big presentation, you find out how it went. You remember. Your remembering says, "What is going on in your life is important to me."

You make a point to remember the courses your child is taking, her teachers, the names of her friends. If your memory isn't good, you write the information down and review it periodically.

You remember the person's favorite color, favorite flower, what they like to eat, the type of books they enjoy reading. If a favorite book of theirs is made into a movie, you bring it up as a subject of conversation. If they complete a project, are awarded a contract, make a big sale, you offer congratulations.

Many men forget their wife's birthday. The wife is crushed. She interprets her husband's forgetfulness as not caring. She says, "He doesn't love me. If he did, he'd remember." A forgotten birthday or anniversary is certainly not the end-all, but it's an indication that a person doesn't love enough.

Some men tell me they're forgetful, and birthdays and special events just don't mean that much to them. I say, "That's because no one has ever missed your birthday, so you don't really understand." I ask, too, how many times they've forgotten a football game? They say that's different. ***Is the difference because one is important and one is not? And which is really important?***

• • •

Saying thank you is another way to remember. For example:

"I love the pin you gave me, Martha. I wear it all the time."

"We had such a good time at the play. Thanks for inviting us."

"Thanks, Don, for taking such good care of me when I was sick."

Right now, look around you. Who do you want to remember to thank?

• • •

Every time I do something special for my niece, Machelle, she sends me the same thank-you card because I enjoy it so much. The card by Gibson features characters from the comic strip *Mother Goose and Grimm*.

"Opportunity is missed by most people because it is dressed in overalls and looks like work."

Thomas Edison

On the front it says, ***"To: Your Royal Thoughtfulness"***
On the inside it reads, ***"From: Your Humble Thankfulness!"***[7]
I've never gotten tired of receiving this card.

I know a man who kept telling his girlfriend he didn't feel appreciated, he didn't think she loved him. She said she did, but when she went on a trip, she rarely brought him a present, even though he took care of many things while she was gone. He's a coffee drinker; she likes tea. In the time they've been together, more than a year and a half, she's failed to furnish her apartment with a coffee pot.

• • •

I was talking to my friend Michaeleen while sucking on a piece of hard candy. All of a sudden Michaeleen looked at me and said, "Doris, can you speak?" I shook my head no. She turned me around and did the Heimlich maneuver several times. Out flew the piece of candy that had lodged in my throat.

In our office when a client reaches a goal, behaves appropriately in a difficult situation or does a kindness, we say, "You get a gold star."

That weekend I went and found a necklace for Michaeleen that had about 20 gold stars on it. It also had some silver ones and some with rhinestones. It's pretty glitzy, I must admit, but Michaeleen frequently wears it. Each time I see her wearing it, I'm reminded of what she did. Each time she wears it, she's reminded of what she did. We remember.

• • •

I've been writing a column for the *St. Louis Post-Dispatch* for 17 years. Often someone will say to me, "I read your column this week." This is love. This is remembering.

I wrote a column about my mother this past year. It was reprinted in many newspapers around the country, and many readers wrote telling me how it brought back memories of their own mothers. Following is the column.

"Ceremonies are different in every country, but true politeness is everywhere the same."

Apples of Gold

"HI MOM. HAPPY BIRTHDAY!

"When I looked on the calendar and found that your birthday fell on the day my column runs, I decided to write my column about you. So sit back, and I hope you enjoy because I'm going to talk about how great you are.

"I think my earliest memory of you, Mom, was when you slipped on the ice on the front steps and couldn't get up. I was three, and you had me go to a neighbor's house to get help. It was you and me in that little house; Dad was away in the war. I remember loving you so hard.

"I remember the day you enrolled me in kindergarten, and I got sick, and you carried me four blocks because I couldn't walk. You were so worried.

"Remember when I would come home for lunch when I was in grade school, and we'd sit at the table and eat soup? We'd listen to "Rex Davis and the News" and then that radio soap opera that started with, "Can a girl from a small mining town in West Virginia...?" I loved coming home for lunch and being with you.

"I remember, too, that every day about four o'clock you'd go wash up and put on make-up because Dad was coming home. I used to secretly admire you as I watched you put on your lipstick. You were so pretty. You still are beautiful, Mom.

"I remember one night I was not a very good girl, and you told me that when the ice cream man came, I was not going to get an ice cream. I was sure you were going to change your mind. You went out to that little truck and got everyone a drumstick but me. I was so sad when you didn't get me one. I knew then I better behave. Thanks, Mom, for having the courage to discipline me.

"I remember all the times you took me to swim practice, and all the malts we drank afterwards. Mom, do you know how many fat grams are in those malts? They were sure good, weren't they?

"Remember all the meals you prepared? Pork chops with mashed potatoes and applesauce and peas. Fried chicken, mashed potatoes, white gravy, spinach, beets and salad. And pie for dessert. And when you made liver for Dad, you made us girls bacon because we couldn't get the liver down.

"Remember how I used to read the Betty Crocker cookbook and cook all summer long? You ate everything I

> ***"Earth is crammed with heaven, and every common bush is afire with God."***
>
> Apples of Gold

made, even my first cherry pie when you had to tear the crust because it was so tough. You were my friend.

"Remember when I had John. I couldn't get him to sleep for anything, and you'd come over and rock him and he'd go to sleep? That's when I realized experience was everything.

"I remember when I started writing my newspaper column 17 years ago. Anna was a baby. If I got writer's block, you'd come over and play with her or take her for a walk so I could get it together.

"I remember, too, all the times you babysat John and Paul, and all the swimming outings and fishing trips you took them on. And how you'd save your money for Christmas to be able to give everyone a special gift.

> ***"What we must decide is perhaps how we are valuable rather than how valuable we are."***
>
> Edgar Friedenberg

"Mom, you have given me so much. You taught me to say "please" and "thank you" and "I'm sorry." You taught me to give hugs and freely say "I love you." You gave me the gift of liking to work. You gave me a belief in God and a religion and you taught me to pray. You gave me the courage to try new things and be adventuresome. You gave me the love of cooking and eating and having family gatherings. You taught me how to take care of others and to be responsible. You taught me to smile and laugh and enjoy life and make each day count. You are a wonderful wife, a sweet grandma, a special human being and my mom. I love you!"

Do you remember? Do you let others know that you remember?

3. Love Is Giving

To love means to give. If you know how to love, you are giving. You give compliments, hugs, kisses, smiles, presents, and cards. You offer counsel, solace and your time.

• • •

Peter was 27 and dying of prostate cancer. He had been working for his company for two years as the assistant buyer for merchandising. He had been off work for three weeks because of surgery and treatment. When he went back to work, the head of the company sat down with Peter and said, "Whatever you need, let us know. You'll get your full pay, no matter what. Just get yourself well."

Peter struggled to go to work, sometimes only a few hours a day. Everyone in his department pitched in and took up the slack. Until the day Peter died, he received a paycheck. The boss and the people in Peter's department knew how to give, how to love.

• • •

One year at Christmas I asked my mother what she would like Santa Claus to bring her. She said without hesitation, "A bicycle." I asked with enthusiasm, "And what kind of a bicycle would you like Santa to bring?" She said she'd like an exercise bicycle. I thought, "Oh darn." I wanted to buy her a real bicycle, one she could pedal around. I knew she didn't have a bike as a child. Maybe she would like to go with me to the store and ride a real bicycle? She said no. What she wanted was one that didn't go anywhere. In the end I got her what she wanted. One of my all-time favorite pictures of Mom is of her smiling happily in a red dress and high heels, perched on her brand new bicycle that didn't go anywhere on Christmas Day.

> ***"Contemplation without action is to be unjust to yourself."***
>
> Conway Stone

Do you give others what they want instead of what you want?

When I do marriage counseling, one of the things I'm most struck with is the lack of generosity between partners. They don't give to each other. The husband doesn't tell his wife she looks nice, or has beautiful eyes, or that he loves her sense of humor. The wife, on the other hand, doesn't remind her husband that she loves his hair, or ruddy complexion, or the fact that he's so darned smart.

When I talk about the importance of giving compliments, I'll often ask the husband to give his wife five compliments right there in the session. He can't do it. He stumbles and stammers, and I have to help him think of nice things to say to the woman he's been living with for years.

When I ask the wife to give her husband five compliments, she's able to do it immediately, but her compliments often have a critical undertone. For example she'll say, "It's nice that you finally got the guttering fixed." Or, "I like your hair now that you've got it cut." Her compliments are prickly. Prickly compliments are not loving.

"To change our perspective in a conflict is to move from a point of view to a viewing point."

The Aiki Approach

• • •

I'm seeing a couple in therapy who recently married. He's 15 years older. They just bought a house. Although he's a multimillionaire, he refuses to put his new wife's name on the house. When I ask him why, he says, "It's my money. I earned it, she didn't. If her name's on the house and we divorce, she'll get half the house."

Another problem this couple has is that she has no children and would like to have a child. He says he's done having children. He has four. She says, "You promised me we would have a baby."

He says, "I changed my mind."

This man is not giving or loving.

• • •

CASE STUDY

A friend complains to me that her mother, now in her mid-eighties, talks almost exclusively about the past.

When my friend tells her mother, "Mom, you've told me that story," her mother says, "I know, but I want to tell you again. It makes me feel better."

I've known the mother for years. She's been a giver all her life. She raised two children and ran a restaurant with her husband. Every day they were up cooking by 6 a.m. When this woman came to her daughter's house for a visit, she'd pitch in and cook, clean and iron. Now age has beaten her down. She's all bent over and can barely walk. She's become forgetful. Perhaps the only thing she can give is her story.

If you are a grown child who feels frustrated by an aging parent's repetitive story, show your love by listening. If you can't bear to hear the same story again, allow yourself to drift and daydream without becoming impatient or annoyed. Remember: The only gift your parent may have to give is her story.

• • •

Love is giving your child's hair a rumple when you pass. Love is bringing your husband a cup of coffee. It's jumping up and taking care of your little ones while your mate sleeps in. It's inviting your folks for dinner. Bringing the office gang donuts on a cold November morning. Visiting someone in a nursing home. Babysitting for a friend's child. Pitching in and helping a colleague at work.

Love is sharing an idea, sharing money, giving time, giving someone a pat, a compliment, a present.

Do you know how to give, how to love?

> ***"Heaven is blessed with perfect rest, but the blessing of earth is toil."***
>
> Apples of Gold

4. Love Is Receiving

Love is being able to receive.

When I was in the third year of writing my newspaper column, a new editor decided to drop my column. The day I found out I was being canceled, I couldn't stop crying. I cried all day, all night and all the next day. The only two people I told were my husband and my partner, Serra. Neither had seen me in such a state. Both of them held me and let me cry. Through my tears I whimpered, "I'm not going to tell anyone."

Serra, the wise mother-of-reason, said, "Doris, people will see that your column isn't in the newspaper. They will ask you about it. Go to the paper and see if there isn't something you can do."

I finally shut off the tears and blew my nose for the hundredth time and decided I just couldn't let this happen. I called the managing editor of the newspaper and made an appointment.

When we talked, he said, "Columns come and go, and readers like new things." I said, "But the column is well read.

It's reprinted in school newsletters; it hangs on company bulletin boards. It helps people in their daily life."

He said, "Have some people write and tell me how much they like the column and we'll reconsider."

I said, "Fine."

I now had the task of asking people to write letters. What I discovered was that I didn't know how to ask for help. I knew about giving. I was a wife, a mother of three children. I was a therapist. I was responsible for training graduate students to do group therapy. I gave talks in the community. I advised my friends. But I didn't know how to receive.

In the next two weeks I learned a lot about humility and asking for help. It was very painful. I asked people to write letters, and a friend got up a petition to save my column. Soon after, the managing editor called me and said, "Okay. You've got your column back."

• • •

> ***"We at Chrysler borrow money the old-fashioned way. We pay it back."***
>
> Lee Iacocca

I think people are adept either at giving or receiving. Mostly it's women who know how to give and men who know how to receive. I no longer judge giving as being better than receiving. I think some people need to receive while others need to give. Difficulties arise, however, when one only receives and has no idea how to give back. Or when one gives and does not know how to receive.

• • •

I know a man who hated to say "I love you" to his wife. When his wife told him "I love you," he became annoyed. When I asked him why he was annoyed, he said, "When she says she loves me it's really for her, because she expects me to say it back."

Certainly he had a point. When we tell someone "I love you," often there's some expectation, some demand, that the person say it back. At the same time, I believe saying "I love you" may be one of the most perfect forms of giving and receiving. When someone says, "I love you," the person is giving. When someone says, "I love you, too," he or she is giving back.

• • •

There's an old rabbinic tale which addresses this issue of giving and receiving.

"The Lord said to the rabbi, "Come, I will show you hell." They entered a room where a group of people sat around a huge pot of stew. Everyone was famished and desperate. Each held a spoon that reached the pot but had a handle so long that it could not be used to reach their mouths. The suffering was terrible.

"Come, now I will show you heaven," the Lord said after a while. They entered another room, identical to the first — the pot of stew, the group of people, the same long spoons. But there everyone was happy and nourished.

"I don't understand," said the rabbi. "Why are they happy here when they were miserable in the other room, and everything was the same?"

The Lord smiled. "Ah, but don't you see? Here they have learned to feed each other."[8]

> *"To change a habit, make a conscious decision, then 'act out' the new behavior."*
>
> Maxwell Maltz

5. Love Is Respecting

If you know how to love, you are respectful. You do not tell someone you will do something and then not do it. You do not make people wait. You return telephone calls. You do not name-call or make sarcastic comments or use a hostile tone of voice. You do not hit, push, try to intimidate or refuse to talk because you are angry. You do not lie or try to dupe another. Nor do you ignore your marriage vows. You treat others with kindness. You are considerate, thoughtful and polite. In your presence, others feel worthwhile and valued.

If you are an employer:

You pay people a fair salary. You do not pile more and more work on them. You recognize their contribution to the company. You provide a healthy and pleasant work environment. You do not lose your temper or degrade an employee. You do not set up a situation wherein people feel threatened and competitive with one another.

> ***"Character is a victory, not a gift."***
> Apples of Gold

If you are an employee:

You don't take advantage of your company. You do not pad your expense account or slough off your job, roam the halls, procrastinate or take too much personal time. You work to the best of your abilities, try hard to get along with everyone and help establish an environment of cooperation.

Ask yourself: ***Am I a respectful boss or employee? In what ways might I improve?***

• • •

A woman told her accountant husband that she wanted to pay off their mortgage. Her parents had lost their home in the Depression, and she didn't want the same thing to happen to them. The husband said that with a mortgage rate of 5.5 percent, it would be better not to pay off the loan. But because his wife felt anxious, he paid it off. He respected his wife more than money.

• • •

My husband runs a company. Sometimes he shares a problem with me. I immediately want to tell him what I think he should do. Instead I ask, "Do you want my feedback or do you want me to simply listen?" Usually he says, "Listen."

I think, "Oh heck." But if I'm being respectful of him, I do what he wants. I listen.

6. Love Is Confronting and Disciplining

If you know how to love, you confront and discipline when necessary. You do not sit by while your mate drinks himself to sleep at night, or your friend gains a lot of weight, or your sister never visits your parents, or your co-worker carries off the company's supplies, or your child always has money and you have no idea where he's getting it. You take the risk and talk with the person.

Unfortunately, if you decide to take charge and confront an individual, you put yourself at risk to have that person turn the confrontation around and become annoyed or angry with you. People have a habit of wanting to "kill the messenger." At the same time, confronting and disciplining are important parts of love, and if you never take the risk, I question how loving you are.

Right now I have a friend who is looking to transfer out of her department because she can't stand her boss. Why? Her boss refuses to take charge. "He never has an opinion," she says. "When we're having a meeting, he lets people talk on and on. And whoever yells the loudest gets his way. The upshot is, everyone feels helpless." Needless to say, this boss is not loving.

> ***"The serious man thinks always of virtue; the common man thinks of comfort."***
>
> Confucius

Here's another example of people who do not know how to confront, how to love.

A woman was getting her license renewed when June walked into the bureau. "Judging by the woman's appearance," said June, "she was close to 80. She was using a cane and had difficulty walking. Another woman, presumably her daughter, had to help her. When the elderly woman got to the counter, she had a hard time understanding what the clerk was asking.

"When it was time for the eye test, she was uncoordinated and had trouble putting her head against the machine. She took at least five minutes to complete the test. Most people finished in 30 seconds. The woman kept saying she couldn't see. Finally the clerk said, 'Okay. Go get your picture taken.'"

The woman who was renewing her license is not loving. The clerk who allowed her to renew her license is not loving. The daughter who helped her mother is not loving.

No one wants to hang up their car keys. Sometimes a person must confront herself, "It's not safe for me to drive." Sometimes a grown child must be the one to say to his parent, "No more driving, Dad. I love you. That's why I can't let you drive." Sometimes a professional, such as a doctor, must take the risk and tell his patient, "No more driving. Your eyes are too bad."

• • •

4

CASE STUDY

In the next story, it was the principal of the school who had the courage to confront.

It was prom time, and some of the high school juniors and seniors chartered a bus to take them to the dance. During the bus ride they drank beer and whiskey. By the time they arrived at the dance, a number of them were drunk.

The school decided to suspend these students for 11 days. The students were allowed to go to the school district's alternative discipline center, where they could work on their assignments under teacher supervision. Several of the students' parents protested the suspensions, complaining that the school was being too harsh.

The parents who protested do not know how to love.

• • •

Liz's mother was in excruciating pain, dying of bone cancer. Liz spent days taking her mother to the hospital for treatment, waiting on her, sitting by her bedside, offering comfort to her father. Liz's husband, Alan, never went to the hospital, never offered to help out. He offered no support to his wife or in-laws.

Some months after Liz's mom died, Alan's mother became ill and needed to be taken to the hospital for treatments. Because Alan's father is in his eighties, the couple needed help. Liz took it upon herself to help.

Alan remained distant from his mother during her illness, as he had from his mother-in-law. Additionally, he chose to go on a two-week ski trip with an old college roommate and the roommate's girlfriend.

When Liz complained to Alan's therapist about Alan's lack of support, the therapist responded, "Alan needs to take care of himself during this period. He's confronting his own mortality."

Liz's response, "What about confronting his responsibility?"

I wonder why the therapist did not confront Alan on his lack of caring for his wife, his in-laws and his own parents. Was it easier for the therapist to be supportive of Alan's fears than confront Alan on his responsibilities? Good therapy requires both.

> ***"It is never too late to expand our horizons."***
> Anonymous

How could Alan justify little to no support to his wife when her mother was dying? And what about supporting his in-laws? I bet through the years they had been there for him some of the time. And his own parents — is there no love for them?

Alan will never be a loving human being until he confronts his own behavior.

• • •

CASE STUDY

Emily, age 16, thought she was too old to have a curfew. She also thought she shouldn't have to report where she was going or who she'd be with. Emily's mother believed differently. She thought it was important to know her daughter's whereabouts and set curfews. Typically, when Emily's mother asked her daughter about plans, the daughter gave her halfway answers and used a "get-out-of-my-life" tone of voice.

Whenever the father heard the two of them bickering, he would say to the mother, "Leave her alone. She's only young once." To his daughter he'd say, "Don't mind her. You know your mother. She's always complaining about something."

Confronting children is love. Teaching them responsibility and manners is love. Having expectations, guidelines and rules is love.

Are you loving enough to your children?
Is there someone you need to be confronting?

7. Love Is Playing

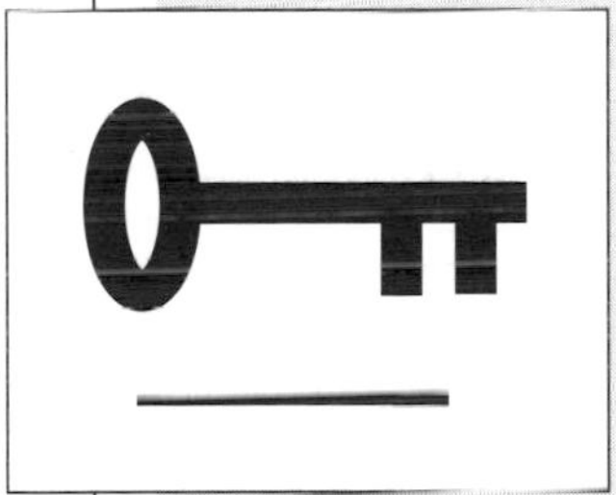

To love means you can play. You take time to enjoy others. You go ice skating, to the movies, to the park. You take a drive, have a picnic, go camping. You gather up the family and go to the zoo.

How much time do you spend playing? Having lunch with co-workers, watching television, reading for pleasure?

How much time do you spend with your mate? Going for walks, having sex, dining out?

How much time do you spend playing with your children?

> ***"Be more concerned with what God thinks about you than what people think about you."***
>
> God's Little Instruction Book

Do you see an imbalance? Do you spend too much time focusing on your own activities while ignoring your mate? Too little time for you, too much for your children?

A man told me his wife would be a good golfer if she would only concentrate and listen to what he said. She shot back, "You get too critical. Even our friends feel sorry for me on the golf course."

He said, "Hasn't your game improved since I've been telling you what to do? And when you play lousy, you come home mad. You're not a stupid woman, but you've got to con-cen-trate. Con-cen-trate." His voice was gruff as he pointedly enunciated his words.

He looked at me and said, "Do you play golf?" I told him I drive the cart and cheer. He dismissed me with, "My poor dear, you don't get it."

Am I the one who doesn't get it?

If a sport makes you miserable, it's not play. If you get angry with others while golfing, playing cards or in a board game, this is not play, nor is it loving. Screaming harshly at your children from the sidelines to "get that ball" is not play, not love.

> ***"The secret of happy living is not to do what you like but to like what you do."***
>
> Apples of Gold

I looked up the word "play" in a thesaurus. What I found was "frolic, rollick, frisk, romp, caper, lark about, flounce, skip, dance, cut up, horse around, fool around, carry on."

Do you skip and lark about with your wife? Romp with your children? Dance with your friend? Cut up with your co-workers?

Do you know how to play? And is your play loving?

8. Love Is Forgiving

To love means you forgive. You forgive your parents for something that happened long ago. You forgive a child for his crankiness. You forgive your mate for a broken promise. You forgive your friend for not caring enough. You forgive your colleague for a hurtful remark. You do not hold tightly to a past hurt. You mend fences and move on with the knowledge that everyone makes mistakes.

• • •

I know a family in which some of the grown siblings stopped talking. Because of an argument, a difference in opinion, two families closed the door on each other forever. I think, "What a tragedy. Was there no one smart enough, tenacious enough, caring enough to forgive?"

• • •

I'm seeing a woman in therapy who over the years has secretly spent more than $35,000 of her family's savings. She is guilt-ridden and remorseful.

How did she spend the money?

If the family went to dinner and the bill was $30, Patty said it was $20. She was fearful that if her husband found out the true cost, he would be angry. When she bought a birthday gift for someone, she lied about the cost. This way she could give what she wanted and not have to face her husband's wrath over the cost of the gift. If they had to buy extra food because they were entertaining, she would supplement the food bill out of savings.

> ***"Forgiveness is a virtue of the brave."***
>
> Gandhi

When Patty's husband learned that she had spent their savings and was secretly taking from his IRA by forging his name, he told her to get out. He immediately filed for divorce.

Patty feels guilty that she took money from their savings. She feels guilty because she did not have the courage to confront her husband about the way he controlled with money. She feels great sadness over the loss of her family. Her biggest hope is that her ex-husband will forgive her and tell her that in many ways she was a good woman, a good wife. Although this would be wonderful, her ex-husband may never have enough love to forgive her. What Patty must do is come to terms with what she did. What she must do is forgive herself.

• • •

When Suzanne told her husband she was going to put some school papers in his briefcase for him to copy for her, he told her to set them on top of his briefcase and he'd take care of it. Suzanne instantly felt something was wrong.

After her husband fell asleep, she looked in his briefcase.

There she found a letter written on a legal pad. It talked of love and commitment. Suzanne felt guilty for not trusting, and tender feelings welled up for her husband. When she turned the page over and continued to read, however, she realized the letter was for another woman.

"My heart started pounding, and I gasped for air," she said. "I thought I was having a heart attack. My crying was so intense I broke a blood vessel in my eye."

"There is no failure except in no longer trying."
Elbert Hubbard

It's been three years since Suzanne learned of her husband's affair. The two of them have been through marriage counseling, group therapy and Retrouvaille, a program designed to help troubled marriages.

Today their marriage is stronger than most. But trust and forgiveness remain a problem for Suzanne. Some days she's able to be forgiving and say to herself, "He didn't have the affair to hurt me. He had it to take care of himself."

Other days, hurt and anger overwhelm her. She thinks, "I was a good wife. Why did he betray me? I'll never be able to forgive."

Suzanne is forgiving her husband. It's just that her forgiveness is happening a little at a time.

• • •

If you're having trouble forgiving, don't keep replaying the hurtful incident in your mind. Don't allow yourself to have imaginary conversations or fights in your head. Discipline yourself. Close off the thoughts. Say a prayer over and over. Sing "The Star Spangled Banner" out loud. It's impossible to sing and think about the past at the same time.

You may find yourself innocently bombarded with hurtful thoughts or images. When a memory comes, don't allow yourself to dwell on it. The past is. Move on to the present. Force yourself to get into the now.

Look around. See your environment. If you're in your office, notice the things on your desk. If you're in the car, study the scenery. If you're in your home, turn on some upbeat music.

Another thing I tell people who are struggling with a past hurt — make a list of the good things the other person has done through the years. This changes your focus and allows a different perspective.

Forgiving is hard work. Often you don't forgive all at once. It's more like chipping away at your guilt or resentment. Sometimes it takes years, perhaps a lifetime. Yet there is almost nothing you can't forgive.

Do You Know How to Love Yourself?

If you truly know how to love, you also know how to love yourself. You listen to your body. If it's tired, you let it rest. You listen to your intuition. I've seen many in therapy who have said, "I knew I shouldn't have married him" or "I knew I shouldn't have taken the job," but they did it anyway. They did not listen or respect themselves enough to follow their intuition.

> ***"No man has more time than I."***
>
> Apples of Gold

Loving yourself means you remember that you like popsicles, popcorn, apricots and peach jam, and you keep them around and treat yourself. You remember to wear your favorite cologne or put on your favorite tie. You remember that as much as you like watching your grandchildren, you get tired and you need backup help if they're to be with you all weekend.

Loving yourself requires that you give to yourself. You look in the mirror and say, "Hi, what a great smile you have. What beautiful eyes you have." You pat yourself on the back for a job well done. Sometimes you take a day off to play.

You love yourself by letting others care for you. You allow yourself to receive. When someone offers to help you with a report, clean your garage or help rebuild your porch, you let them. You have learned to feel comfortable letting others help you out.

To love yourself means you are respectful of yourself. You don't give yourself to someone sexually so he will like you. You don't go to a party and drink too much. If you have a drinking problem, you go to AA, or Rational Recovery, or a treatment program, or a therapy group. If you're overweight, you exercise and eat differently. Your list of things to do for the day is reasonable. You do not put it on yourself to run to the nursing home every day to take care of a parent. You give yourself certain days off each week. You pursue goals and know your limitations.

You care enough about yourself to confront yourself on behavior that you need to change. You stay home from work and go to the doctor when you're ill. You take time to play a little every day. You forgive yourself.

A Lifetime to Love

Learning to love takes a lifetime. Most people know how to love in some areas but not in others. A father may be wonderful at giving to his children but not good at disciplining. A wife may be giving to her children but not giving to her husband. A man may be forgiving toward his family but not respectful of his co-workers. Parents may provide the best money can buy for their children but never listen to their hopes and fears.

> ***"What we are is God's gift to us; what we become is our gift to God."***
>
> Anonymous

Love is listening, remembering, giving, receiving, respecting, confronting and disciplining, playing and forgiving.

Do you know how to love yourself and others?

CHAPTER 5

Do You Get Too Angry?

5

> ***"He who strikes the first blow confesses he has run out of ideas."***
>
> Apples of Gold

Many people get too angry. If someone says or does something they don't like, they become angry. They may handle their anger by getting a mean look on their face, using a threatening tone or raising their voice. They may make rude comments, shout obscenities and degrade the person who they think has crossed them. Or the angry person may simply shut another out, pout, refuse to talk or even acknowledge another's existence, sometimes for days on end.

When I see an individual trying to bully another with his anger, I wonder: "Doesn't he understand how hurtful he's being?" I also think, "How can he justify such meanness?"

In the following stories you will meet many people who have problems with their anger. As you read, ask yourself: ***Do I act like this person?***

• • •

"Jim wanted to get a dog," said his wife. "He pushed to get a dog. But I was hesitant. I knew from past experience that Jim probably wasn't going to be much help. But in the end I agreed, and we got a dog.

"When the dog didn't behave the way Jim thought she should, like when she had accidents on the carpet, Jim would take her outside and beat her. Naturally the dog became afraid of him, so Jim refused to take care of the dog.

> *"People who fly into a rage always make a bad landing."*
>
> Apples of Gold

"If I had to go out of town, I'd have to take the dog to a kennel. Once I had to leave on short notice and I forgot to make arrangements. Jim called me that night and was furious that the dog was there. He said, 'I sure hope you're coming home tonight because I'm not going to take care of this dog. She'll just have to go without food and water until you get home.' There I was over 250 miles away, feeling helpless.

"Not too long after the dog incident, Jim asked me to tape a show for him on the VCR. Somehow I missed the first half hour. When he went to play the tape, he was outraged. He kept screaming at me, 'I can't count on you for anything. You're so stupid.' He then took the tape and ripped it up, yelling, 'Now no one can watch it.'"

If you met Jim, you would probably like him. Responsible, educated, articulate, funny, good-looking and sometimes very generous and kindhearted. But if something doesn't go his way, he becomes mean and aggressive.

• • •

CASE STUDY

A man and wife came to me for marriage counseling. It was their first session. I started by asking each of them if they wanted to stay married. The woman nodded her head and said yes. The man asked me what the hell that meant.

I explained that sometimes people come for marriage counseling and they're not sure if they want to stay married. They have reservations. Other times one of them wants out of the marriage. The way a person answers this question gives me a good deal of information — how I'll focus the session, which spouse is most unhappy, who at that moment has the leverage and if marriage counseling is even appropriate for them.

After my explanation I asked the man what *he* saw as the main problem in his marriage. He said, "Communication." He then screwed up his face, turned toward his wife and said sarcastically, "My wife doesn't talk to me. She doesn't think I'm good enough to talk to."

I said to him, "You're getting too angry."

His response, "You're damn right I'm angry." Then he attacked me. His words were, "And who do you think you are asking me if I want to stay married? I'm getting out of here and seeing somebody who knows what they're doing."

With that announcement, he jumped up and stomped out of the office.

Needless to say, this man has an anger problem.

Face It — Do You Get Too Angry?

You know if you get too angry. You might not like to admit it. You may downplay your anger's intensity and frequency. But you know if you have an anger problem. What you may not understand is what drives your anger, the consequences of getting too angry or what you can do to change.

The No. 1 Reason You Get Angry — You Think Negative Thoughts

The No. 1 reason you respond with anger is that you think negative thoughts. When an event happens, instead of putting a neutral or positive interpretation on it, you put a negative interpretation on it. By thinking negative thoughts, you actually create your own anger. You can give meaning to an event in less than a second. Within a few seconds you can have a number of negative thoughts.

When Lou walked into his kitchen one afternoon and saw a stack of college books on the table and a schedule with his wife's name on it, he became furious. Lou's negative thought — his wife was going back to school to get an education so she could divorce him. It was the way Lou interpreted the situation — the books, the schedule — that created his anger.

If I had walked into the kitchen with Lou that day, I wouldn't have responded with anger. Instead I would have thought, "Oh, someone's going to school." This is a neutral thought. I might have read the titles of the books with interest. But I would not have felt angry.

• • •

Suppose you tell your daughter you want her to clean the kitchen while you're gone. She says okay. A few hours

> ***"Anger is never without a reason, but seldom a good one."***
>
> Benjamin Franklin

later you come home, and the kitchen is still a mess. You immediately think a negative thought — "I can't count on her for anything." Your next negative thought: "She never does anything around here that I tell her." Rapidly followed by a third negative thought: "What a brat; she's never going to amount to anything." In less than a second you have had three negative thoughts and you're angry.

Now let's examine more closely what happened. First, you asked your daughter to clean the kitchen, and she agreed. Several hours later when you came home, the kitchen was not clean. You have no further information. All the other thinking you did was conjecture and negative.

Because in the past your daughter has often agreed to do something and then not followed through, you *assume* that she didn't clean the kitchen because she was talking on the telephone or watching television. But you really don't know.

"When a man has a 'pet peeve,' it's remarkable how often he pets it."

Apples of Gold

Maybe the neighbor had an emergency, and she ran over to watch the neighbor's child. Maybe her girlfriend hit a deer with her car, came by the house to call the police, and in the commotion your daughter didn't have a chance to clean the kitchen.

I bet you're thinking, "Oh sure, her friend hit a deer."

Well, my daughter's friend hit a deer and she did come by our house to call the police. So it's not impossible. Until you have all the information, you're making assumptions that heat you up until you're raging.

Without these negative thoughts, you'd be the first to admit that sometimes your daughter does do chores around the house. In fact, just yesterday she mowed the lawn and helped fold laundry. And, yes, sometimes she doesn't follow through on her promises. But do you really think she's never going to amount to anything?

The No. 2 Reason You Get Angry — You Perceive a Threat

Along with thinking negative thoughts when things don't go the way you expect, you feel thrown off balance, threatened, challenged, not in control of the situation.

Going back over the previous examples:

Jim, the guy who refused to take care of the dog, felt confused and off balance when he walked in and saw the dog. Things were not the way he imagined they would be. He had not expected the dog to be at home. He also was threatened because he had to deal with a dog who didn't like him. When he discovered that his wife hadn't recorded the show properly, his plans were interrupted. His world wasn't the way it was supposed to be.

Lou, the man who overreacted to the college books, was thrown off guard when he saw the books. He felt a vague sense that he was losing control. When he made a negative interpretation that his wife was going to get her degree and leave him, his fear increased.

The man who walked out of marriage counseling felt threatened because he was in an uncomfortable situation, and I had challenged him about his anger.

The No. 3 Reason You Get Angry — You Have a Physiological Response

Once you put a negative interpretation on an event, which takes less than a second, you have an immediate physiological response. Adrenalin rushes through your bloodstream, your heart beats faster, your respiration increases, your blood pressure goes up, your skin temperature rises and sugar is released into your bloodstream. You're ready to do battle.

Many professionals think that the rush of adrenalin causes you to believe that it is the actions of others that make you feel angry. But this is not so. Your anger is a result of the way you interpret the event and the fact that you feel threatened in some way.

It Takes Three Ingredients

Again, your anger is the result of a combination of three factors happening within a split second.

1. You put a negative interpretation on an event.

2. You perceive a threat or judge that you've been challenged.

3. You have an adrenalin rush.

If you put a negative interpretation on an event but do not perceive a threat, you will not feel angry. For example, you may hear on the evening news that someone walked into a local bank and opened fire, killing nine people. Certainly you're going to interpret this event as negative. You might say, "Nobody is safe." But because you do not feel a threat yourself, you do not feel angry.

If you have an adrenalin rush without a negative thought you may feel anxious, jealous, sad, or great joy. The hormone adrenalin fuels all of our emotions. But it's our thinking that determines what emotion we are feeling.

Some people are extremely resistant to believing their anger is generated by what they think. What they want to believe is that other people cause their anger. If you hold to the notion that it is others that cause your anger, you're not as responsible for it. It's the old, "he made me do it" excuse. But if you come to understand that your anger is generated by what you think, the way you interpret an event, you are definitely responsible.

"A soft answer turns away wrath, but a harsh word stirs up anger."

Proverbs 15:1

Things You Do to Make Your Anger Burn Hotter

In addition to interpreting an event in a negative way, you have other thoughts that help you rev up your anger. These include name-calling, exaggerating and using a should-and-ought belief system.

You Name-Call

You would probably admit in your off-anger hours that most people are not all good or all bad, but a combination. Even the most vicious person can at times show kindness and compassion. And the kindest, most loving person can exhibit very mean behavior.

When you're angry with someone, however, you put him in the bad-guy category, and you label him. You call him a jerk, an idiot, a brat, a bastard or whatever colorful noun comes to mind. Once you've labeled the person, he loses his humanity. He becomes the label you've put on him, and he's now your enemy.

> ***"I used to get mad and blow my top — a Donald Duck-type thing."***
>
> Walt Disney

What is the name you call others when you're angry? Most people have one or two favorites.

You Exaggerate

Along with name-calling, you exaggerate the seriousness of the event. Because Jim's wife didn't tape the show properly, he tells her she's stupid and can't do anything right. When Lou sees his wife's college books, he also sees divorce papers coming.

You Think in Terms of Shoulds and Oughts

You have a belief system about how people should act, right? And when people don't do what *you think they should,* you become righteous and indignant. You fuel your anger by running out a lot of shoulds and oughts. For example, Jim thinks, "She should have put that stupid dog in the kennel." "She ought to know how to use the VCR!"

5

C A S E S T U D Y

When People Interpret Events Differently

When presented with an event, any event, you make an interpretation. If you interpret the event negatively, you are likely to burn hot. If you interpret the event more neutrally, you will not feel angry.

For instance, a man told me that he and his wife had gone out of town for the weekend and somehow there was a misunderstanding on the part of the wife's grown children about when the couple would return. When the couple came home and listened to their answering machine, they found that the children had left a number of messages such as "Where are you?" "We're trying to reach you" and "Call us as soon as you get home."

Immediately the man thought, "Why don't those kids leave their mother alone? They're so demanding." Along with these negative thoughts, he felt threatened — his life was once again being interrupted by these children. Within less than a second of hearing the messages and making his interpretation, this man had a rush of adrenalin. His heart started pounding, and his blood pressure went up. He then interpreted the rush he felt as anger because the children had called so often.

When the woman heard the messages on the machine, she immediately thought, "The kids must have been worried sick that something happened to us. I guess I didn't make it clear to them when we were coming home." Along with these thoughts, this woman also had a rush of adrenalin. Her heart started pounding, and her blood pressure went up. She interpreted the rush she felt as anxiety over having caused her children so much concern.

Because the man interpreted the rush he felt as anger, he was tempted to say something negative about the children to his wife. Because the woman interpreted the rush she felt as anxiety over having put the children through unnecessary worry, she wanted to immediately telephone them and reassure them that all was well.

"The really happy man is the one who can enjoy the scenery when he has to take a detour."

Apples of Gold

A Thinking-It-Through Exercise

To help incorporate what you have read and to understand that your anger is primarily the result of your thinking, answer the following questions.

1. In the past week what situation or event occurred where you became angry?

____

____

____

____

2. When the situation occurred, what negative thoughts did you have?

____

____

____

____

3. What neutral thoughts might you have had instead?

____

____

____

____

4. Had you had neutral thoughts instead of negative ones, would you have felt angry?

____

____

____

____

What's Your Anger Style? An Anger-In or an Anger-Out?

"A good memory is fine — but the ability to forget is the true test of greatness."
Apples of Gold

A person usually has several styles of anger. An anger-out style shows up as yelling, shouting, ranting, raving, kicking the furniture and slamming doors. An anger-in style is displayed by pouting, sulking, holding a grudge, refusing to talk and withdrawing.

Carl, the boss, asked Rosie if she knew anything about data communication. Rosie said she didn't know much but would look into it. When Carl reviewed Rosie's time sheets two weeks later and found she had put in 20 hours researching data communication, Carl went ballistic. He ranted and raved and wanted to know what the hell she was doing. This was not what she should have been working on!

Rosie also became furious. She, however, said nothing. She got her car keys and left work. The next three days she called in sick. Two weeks later she gave notice that she was leaving the company.

Carl's anger style that day was anger-out. When he saw Rosie's time sheets, he had negative thoughts, felt threatened, had a rush of adrenalin and, unfortunately, gave himself permission to blow.

Rosie's anger style was anger-in. When Carl confronted her on her time sheets, she had negative thoughts, felt threatened, had a rush of adrenalin and, unfortunately, closed up like a clam and withdrew.

How About You?

1. Are you an anger-out or an anger-in when you're at work?

2. What about when you're at home with family?

3. How about with someone in authority?

4. How about with a co-worker?

Unfortunately, neither of these styles, anger-out or anger-in, is productive. The best style? Control your anger.

5

A Predisposition to Be Angry

Some research suggests that you have inherited a predisposition, a temperament, to be angry. You have inherited emotionality that makes you react intensely to events. And you have inherited an impulsivity so that you respond instantly to an event. But Carol Tavris, in her book *ANGER, The Misunderstood Emotion*, explains,

"Any inherited predispositions we have are more diffuse and generalized than those of lower animals: genes merely provide us with a reaction range, and environmental events determine where in the range an individual will fall." [9]

> ***"All men fall. The great ones get back up."***
>
> Mike Murdock

Just because you are more emotional and excitable than someone else, you don't have to have a bad temper. You may have to work a little harder to control your feelings. But your anger is your anger, and pouting for days or blowing your top because you don't like something is still inappropriate behavior.

Were Your Parents Angry? What About the People You're with Every Day?

Sometimes a person who has an anger problem was raised in a family where one or both parents had a problem with their anger. Certainly if a child sees a parent blowing his top or refusing to talk when things don't go his way, the child is likely to imitate that behavior.

It's also possible that no one made you accountable for your temper as a youngster. No one took you on, made you go to your room or, more important, taught you to look at a situation from several perspectives. You may even have been rewarded for your angry outbursts. Perhaps it was just easier to give you what you wanted than to put up with your temper tantrums.

Having parents who were too angry may be the reason you adopted this behavior. But do you follow everything you were taught?

Another way to develop an anger problem — you live or work with people who are like teakettles. They go around hissing, spitting steam and frequently blowing their tops. Because of the Werther Effect (people decide how to behave based on how others around them are behaving), you have become accustomed to rattling, hissing and blowing your top.

More Research on Anger

Here are some additional findings on anger that may help you become more determined than ever to control this emotion.

- People express anger because it has an effect. Anger is a learned strategy to get your way. It is not a biological inevitability.

- Expressing your anger by raising your voice and yelling does not reduce your anger. In fact, expressing anger frequently intensifies the feeling.

- The more often you give yourself permission to get angry, the more things you'll find to be angry about. Anger builds anger. And expressing anger regularly makes you a hostile person.

- You may actually feel better inside after you rant and rave because you have lessened your physiological arousal — your heart doesn't pound as fast, and your blood pressure drops. What's important to note here, however, is that ranting and raving to lessen your physiological arousal level is a learned cathartic habit. You can get the identical effect of lessening your physiological arousal by taking a brisk walk, listening to music or talking to a friend on the telephone.

- Expressing anger undermines your self-esteem, as well as the self-esteem of the person whom you have chosen as your target. It also diminishes your dignity.

- People who are quick to express anger are generally less tolerant and flexible than those who keep their anger in check.

"To be wronged is nothing unless you continually remember it."

Apples of Gold

- Women express anger every bit as well as men. Men do, however, pout more and hold grudges longer.

- You're more likely to be an anger-out with your mate, children and co-workers; people you see as equal or less important than you. You're more likely to be an anger-in with your boss, banker, lawyer, doctor — people you view as having more power than you.

- The most popular place for people to allow themselves angry outbursts — at home. The place where they are most conscious of controlling their anger — in the workplace. (If you can control your temper at work, you can choose to control it at home.)

Facing Up to Your Anger

I have been guilty of too much anger in the past. I used to get angry when I couldn't find my keys. I'd race around the house yelling, "I can't find my keys. Where are my keys? Help me find my keys." I expected everyone to drop what they were doing and look for my keys.

I'd be angry when the cleaners didn't get a spot out of a blouse or broke a button. I'd get angry at parents who didn't discipline their children at church or a workman who failed to show up.

> ***"A diamond is a piece of coal that stuck to the job."***
>
> Apples of Gold

One memory that stands out is with our older son. Each morning I would drive the boys to school. Almost invariably John would forget his lunch. Because the school didn't have a cafeteria, I was faced with deciding whether to go back home for his lunch and be late for my first appointment or let him go without lunch.

Sometimes I would take him to school with no lunch. Other times I would drive home and we'd pick up the lunch. Regardless of the decision I made, however, I would rant and lecture that little kid all the way to school. "Why can't you be more responsible? You can remember your hockey stick and roller skates. Why can't you remember your lunch?"

He's grown now, and I've apologized to him a number of times for my ugliness. He says, "Come on, Mom. Forget it. You were a good mom."

I'm not going to forget it, though. I want to remember that this kind of anger is not okay. There are other ways to handle problems without getting angry. For instance, I could have remembered his lunch and helped him learn responsibility in a different way.

Getting in Control

Perhaps because I had to work on my anger, I've become quite successful at helping others learn to control theirs. I don't believe you have to experience every pain to be able to help, but sometimes it gives you an edge.

> ***"What wound ever healed but by degrees?"***
> Shakespeare

Almost always, when I see someone who has an anger problem, I suggest the following techniques. If you use them, you will be controlling your anger instead of allowing your anger to control you.

One of the most important and neglected aspects of learning to control your temper is that you must go into training. You have to condition yourself *before* you are presented with an anger-provoking situation, because within a second of feeling crossed, you're already off the anger scale. That's why telling someone to count to 10 or 100 before she reacts doesn't work for an angry person. It only works for people who don't have a problem with their anger.

You would never think of running a marathon without preparing for it. It's the same with anger. You must work to control it before the anger-provoking event occurs.

"I Choose Not to Be Angry"

The first and most important technique I teach: Say to yourself 3,000 times a day: ***"I choose not to be angry, I choose to be in control."*** Say this sentence a few times right now. ***I choose not to be angry, I choose to be in control.***

Say this phrase on and off during the day. Start when you put your feet on the floor in the morning. Repeat it in the shower, as you're brushing your teeth, as you're sitting in traffic, when you're on break. Any time you're doing a mindless task, repeat the phrase to yourself. It will take you about an hour and a half each day. This may sound like too much work. But if you want to control your anger, you must be willing to put in the energy. Remember, too, that you're saying this phrase in your head while doing other activities.

Within three days you'll notice a remarkable change in yourself. When presented with a situation that would ordinarily have you red-faced and boiling, you'll respond differently.

Here is what you can expect. Someone will cross you. You'll immediately think an angry thought such as, "How dare she." This thought, which took less than a second, will be followed by a physiological rush. At the same time, if you've been doing your homework every day, your affirmation will pop into your head — *"I choose not to be angry, I choose to be in control."* Immediately, you'll cut off the negative thoughts, you'll calm down, and reason will prevail.

An additional word of caution about this technique: Saying this phrase 300 or 500 times a day won't do it. You've got to say it about 3,000 times. How do I know? Because I came up with this technique 20 years ago, and it has never failed anyone who has used it as directed.

People who are married to someone with a bad temper say they can *feel* when their mate is getting ready for an angry explosion. If your mate can detect that you're going to blow, so can you. When you start that stream of negative thoughts because the house is a mess or your mate overspent, start using your affirmation. The constant repetition of your affirmation will have a calming effect on you. Also get your mind on something else. Clean the kitchen with a vengeance. Practice your golf swing. Take a walk. Telephone a friend.

> ***"Forgiveness makes a future possible."***
>
> Mike Murdock

"X" Marks the Deed

A second suggestion is to put an X on your calendar each time you allow yourself to pout or fly into a rage. Marking down the times you've become angry will make you accountable. You also can see how many days you've made yourself miserable because of your anger.

5

There Is No Box Inside You Labeled "Anger"

Since the mid-1960s many health care professionals have preached that it's healthy to express your anger. Research shows something very different, however. Expressing anger is no more healthy than not expressing it. In addition, expressing anger regularly may be harmful to your health. And we know that repeatedly expressing anger in any relationship does more harm than good.

When I read, "You need to get out your anger," I think, this is bad advice. There is no storage box marked "Anger" inside you. It is your thoughts that generate your anger. If you think about an event where you felt trod upon or victimized, you will feel angry. But it's *your* thinking that generates the feeling.

On occasion, you may want to talk about an incident where every time you think about it, you get yourself all hot and bothered. If you decide to talk about it, however, go into the discussion expecting to hear a different view. Don't expect the other person to accept your interpretation of the event. Sometimes talking leads to more understanding, particularly when both people have their brains turned on and their feelings in check.

Is There Ever a Time to Be Angry?

This question — Is there ever a time to be angry? — has been debated for centuries. Some philosophers and moralists say yes, others say no, many hedge.

I think yes, it is OK to be angry on occasion. And sometimes puffing up and getting angry is helpful to get a point across. Always, however, you should be in control of your anger and it should be coupled with reason. So perhaps the better question might be: How much anger is OK and under what circumstances?

If your little one runs into the street, you'll want to look ferocious and tell him that he cannot go into the street. If

> ***"Do not wait for the last judgment; it takes place every day."***
>
> Bruce Barton

your daughter ventures into an unsafe neighborhood with her friends on Friday night, you'll want to get angry to impress upon her your concern and the possible consequences of her actions. If your 15-year-old son comes home drunk, you'll want to reinforce your words with anger. If your spouse decides not to honor his marriage vows, you'll want to impress on him how you feel trod upon. If your co-worker procrastinates and doesn't complete his part of the project, which keeps you from meeting deadline, you'll want to let him know you're angry. At the same time, in all these instances, you will want to run the show with your thinking, not your feelings.

I think the words of St. Augustine also bear remembering:

"It is better to deny entrance to just and reasonable anger than to admit it, no matter how small it is. Once let in, it is driven out again only with difficulty. It comes in as a little twig and in less than no time it grows big and becomes a beam."[10]

Remember Anger's Consequences

Continually getting angry sets the stage for people to fear and dislike you. Your anger is too hard on their self-esteem. It's also hard on your self-esteem because you probably don't feel good about your behavior.

Your anger creates a situation where people don't trust you because they're never quite sure when you'll turn on them. Your anger closes out love. It's impossible to love another when you're angry, and no one else can love you.

When you're done with your tantrum or your prolonged pouting, and you think back on the way you behaved, you probably feel guilty and a little foolish. You also have the additional job of patching things up. This gets harder and harder, however, because those around you don't believe that this is your last tantrum.

Ask yourself the following:

- ***Why would I continue a behavior that plays havoc with my self-esteem and the self-esteem of others?***

- ***Why would I want people to fear me, dislike me, not trust me, not love me, not respect me?***

With conditioning and work, you can control your anger.

CHAPTER 6

How Do You Handle Suffering and Disappointment?

No one escapes life without pain and disappointment. This is the first noble truth that Buddha taught. Life is pain. Life is suffering.[11]

I look around me. Every person I know has had pain — physical pain and emotional pain. Do you know anyone who has escaped it? I think not.

In the following stories you will hear of pain that others have had to face. Through their stories you will gain insight into the ways you have handled your own disappointments and pain. I believe, too, that as you read about the ways others deal with their suffering, you will see that they have found some answers.

"It's not what happens to us that counts, it's our reaction to it."

Anonymous

CASE STUDY

She's Had a Headache for 10 Years

Amanda has had a headache for over 10 years. Every day she's in pain. She started having frequent headaches in 1984. By 1988, they were daily occurrences. In the beginning Amanda attributed her headaches to stress. She had three teenagers, a busy preschooler and a demanding full-time job as a graphic designer. She took a lot of over-the-counter medication and tried to ignore her aching head.

"In the morning when I opened my eyes there was pain," she said. "On the way to the shower I'd be taking my medication. I'd think, 'I'll get in the shower, and my headache will get better.'

"Then I'd think, 'I'll eat something and it will get better.'

"I'd get to work and think, 'I'll get a cup of coffee and it will get better.'

"I'd then say to myself, 'It's not getting better, but maybe after I eat lunch.'

"Finally I couldn't ignore my headaches any longer."

Amanda's internist sent her to biofeedback sessions with a psychotherapist and to a psychiatrist.

"The psychiatrist tried some of this medication, and more of that, and less of this," she said. "Nothing worked."

She went to a university pain-management program. There Amanda worked with a physical therapist, who helped her with upper back exercises, thinking the problem was muscular. They also had her go to an aerobics class three times a week. Nothing worked.

She had sinus surgery because her sinus cavity was misshapen, and the doctors thought perhaps that was causing the problem. "My sinus surgery was the most painful experience I've ever had," she related. "Worse, it didn't help the headaches.

"I know God will not give me anything I can't handle. I just wish that he didn't trust me so much."

Mother Theresa

"I went to several eye doctors to make sure the problem wasn't visual. I saw my dentist for the possibility of temporomandibular joint dysfunction. I had two MRIs and a CAT scan.

"I went to a special headache clinic. They put me on a tyramine-free diet and presently regulate my medication. But I still have the constant pain.

"Sometimes I think if a doctor told me to get up on the table and bark like a dog, I'd do it.

"I've had acupuncture. I've seen allergists, chiropractors, a reflexologist, a hypnotherapist and several massage therapists. I've even visited a psychic. I've used relaxation techniques. I've had medication in every category that is prescribed for headaches. I've counseled with my minister. I'm now attending a therapy group to keep me from getting discouraged."

A year and a half ago Amanda had to take a permanent leave of absence from her job.

When I asked Amanda how she deals with the pain, she started crying. Along with her tears she half laughed and said, "Well, I cry. The only problem with crying is that it makes my head hurt more."

She also said, "I go to bed with an icepack. I read books on headaches. I do neck-stretching exercises. I pray about 100 times a day saying, 'Please, God, take this pain, I've had enough.' I get mad at my headache and push myself to do housework or take my daughter to gymnastics. I take hot showers that beat on my head. My family gives me head and neck massages. At this point I'm willing to do anything that seems reasonable. I'm waiting for the miracle."

I've known Amanda for 15 years, before she was married, before she had her baby, before she got her first design job. I love Amanda. Sometimes in a childish way I say, "Okay, God, I'll take Amanda's headache today. Give her a day off."

But that's not the way it works. We can't take another person's pain away. We can stand by them and give comfort and support. Sometimes our efforts can take the edge off their pain. But in the end, everyone must face his or her own pain — the pain of a mate's infidelity, a demotion, a broken bone, infertility, chronic illness, not making the team, a poor complexion, having a body type that our society puts down, a lost friendship, the death of a parent, the pain of unloving children.

• • •

"I loved my boss," said Marie. "She was respected by everyone. She thought highly of my work. She thought I was smart. Then my boss left the area, and I was assigned a new boss. This boss is unbelievably difficult to work with. She acts as though I'm stupid and I can't do anything right. She's always on my case about something. Not a day goes by when she doesn't make some snide remark or send me a memo that implies I'm an imbecile.

"I like what I do and I don't want to quit my job, but my job is very stressful because of this woman. The way I cope — I try to ignore her rude comments. Sometimes I get very determined and I put in extra hours trying to please her, to show her what a good worker I am. I tell myself, 'I'm a good person no matter what she thinks.' Sometimes I call my sister in the evening and complain to her. I count the people on the job who like me, and once in a while I go to lunch with my old boss and feel good about myself."

• • •

"All things are possible to him who believes."

Jesus Christ

Jake copes with a different kind of pain.

Jake's wife left him and is pursuing a divorce.

"At first I thought my wife was ridiculous and was being too influenced by a friend who recently divorced. But through my therapy group I've come to see how difficult I've been to live with.

"I've done a lot of crying. A lot of soul searching. Talking to other people. Reading books. My group has been setting me straight, telling me I get too angry and that I'm too controlling. I've lost my wife, but I believe I'm becoming a better person."

• • •

CASE STUDY

Greg, a television personality, was strung along for months by the station he worked for. Were they going to renew his contract or not? The day his contract was to expire, his station offered him a new contract. The job would be the same, but the pay would be significantly less. Greg said he was a good anchor and he had more respect for himself than to sign such a contract. Regretfully, he resigned.

When a newspaper reporter asked him about the pain of losing such a visible job in the community, Greg said he'd been through pain before. And there was no pain that could compare to the pain he had felt when he held his dying 16-year-old in his arms.

Physical pain, emotional suffering: how do people cope? What have they learned? How do they go on?

Amanda handles her pain by trying various options. She goes to one doctor, gives the treatment five or six months and then moves on. She talks to people, picking their brains to see if they've heard of something she hasn't. Sometimes she bulldozes her way through the day, trying to ignore the pain and to focus on someone else. She listens to a problem her husband is having and cooks a meal for a sick friend. She weeds the garden. She uses prayer to give her hope. And sometimes she gives in to her pain and allows herself to tune out the world and go to bed.

Marie tries to deal with the pain of having a difficult boss by working hard, by trying to ignore the rude comments her boss makes, by complaining to her sister, by telling herself she's a good person, and by giving weight to those who do like her.

Jake is dealing with his pain by trying to understand what went wrong in his marriage and changing himself. He goes to therapy, he reads, he listens to others.

Greg deals with his hurts by comparing them to the pain he feels over his son's death. All hurts pale in comparison.

Allowing Disappointments to Take Over Your Life

Sadly, some individuals obsess on their disappointments. They have a financial disaster, or they flunk out of school, or a mate leaves and they can't seem to move beyond the event. They can't or won't let their disappointment go.

Margaret's husband walked out on her and their three children 10 years ago. The week his company announced that he would be made president, he moved out and filed for divorce. Three months later he moved across the country with his secretary to take his new position. Margaret was devastated. Her whole life was upside down. She was forced to dig in and finish raising the children as a single parent. Margaret had to go through the humiliation of being left, change her view of what her future life would be, and quiet her love for her husband.

"In releasing old ways and letting go of the past, we do not lose the good we have gained."

Anonymous

6

Margaret has done a yeoman's job with her children. She's moved to a new neighborhood, made new friends, taken up walking, has a job she enjoys and is dating several men. Outwardly she appears to have moved on with her life, dealt with her sadness.

If you talk to her, however, you will hear her talking of her ex-husband. You will hear her ask, "How could a man just pack up and leave his family?" If you spend any time with her, you'd think her ex-husband left her six months ago, not 10 years ago.

Many people, particularly women, get caught up in blaming and not being able to let go of a mate who rejected them. The reason: many women are outer-focused. They are forever thinking of their mate. They have conversations with him in their head. If he leaves, they don't stop thinking and talking to him. They simply change the subject of their internal conversations. This is why their pain continues. Their outside life is drastically different, but the subject of their internal focus remains the same.

• • •

CASE STUDY

Louis was fired 12 years ago. He was a good employee, but a new regime came in and he was part of the old one. He found a different job, but he has never been able to find one as high paying or as prestigious as his old job. Every conversation you have with Louis contains derogatory remarks about how his old company mistreated him. When I talk with him, I think, "He's suffered enough. Why does he choose to keep fighting with 'them' in his head, making himself miserable?"

I know his other job made him feel worthy and good about himself. And when he lost that job, he lost a lot of his self-respect. I know, too, that his fight with the company is about respecting himself. What Louis fails to understand is that he's causing himself more grief and pain by keeping the fight going in his head.

Margaret and Louis are each classic examples of people who are still suffering from events of long ago. They responded to the painful situation by doing what they needed to do to get their life on track, but they failed themselves by continuing to fight in their head. Inadvertently, they have continued their pain.

• • •

Take a few minutes to think about yourself, and answer the following questions.

- Are you fighting with anyone in your head over a past injustice?

  ____

  ____

- How did that person hurt or disappoint you?

  ____

  ____

- Are you waiting for the person to tell you he made a mistake and you're a worthy, good human being?

  ____

  ____

- When do you think he will call?

  ____

  ____

- How long are you prepared to wait?

  ____

  ____

"To everything there is a season, a time for every purpose under heaven."

Ecclesiastes

6

"I Don't Let Myself Think About It Too Much"

I was talking with a man about his 12-year-old daughter who was killed in an auto accident two years ago. I asked him what he does to keep the pain of his daughter's death from consuming him. He said, "I choose the time to think about her each day. It's usually in the morning when I'm at church. Then I don't let myself think about her anymore that day. If a thought comes that is about her, I push it away. I don't allow myself to go over the details of the accident, or when the police came to get me, or when I went to the hospital to identify her. I couldn't handle it. I shut it out. I concentrate on my wife and our other children.

"I loved her so much. Oh, it hurts. But I can't let myself dwell on it."

CASE STUDY

"This Is Too Big for Me to Handle, God"

"My husband used to fly the kids back to school when they were in college," a mother explained. "My daughter Stacy was in her senior year. My son was a sophomore. There was another girl in the plane. My husband was the pilot. They ran into bad weather 15 minutes before they were to land, and the plane went down. It was Thanksgiving weekend.

"The other family, who lost their daughter, found out before I did. They called my parish priest, and he called me. When I heard, I went outside. I looked up in the sky and kept saying to God, 'You made a mistake. You made a mistake.' Stacy had just sent in her paperwork to be a missionary.

"I also said, 'This is too big for me to handle, God. Now you must take care of me.' After I said that, a prayer shot through my head: 'May the body and blood of our Lord Jesus Christ, being offered in all the tabernacles of the whole world, bring me, not condemnation, but heal my mind and body.'

"I repeated that prayer over and over. As people talked to me about the accident, I kept repeating that prayer. I also prayed for my daughter and son and husband. I said, 'Lord, Jesus, have mercy on them.'

"I knew I would be okay. I closed the family office-supply business and went back to teaching. I stayed only a semester and then opened up a Catholic bookstore.

"People send people to me who are having problems. People who are desperate. I give them that prayer.

"Saying that prayer after the plane accident I knew I could handle it, I could make it. People would come up to me and say, 'I couldn't do it,' and I would console them. It is my faith that has gotten me through this.

"Of course everyone kept telling me to get help, see a therapist. I said, 'My psychiatrist is upstairs.'"

"I Forced Myself to Stay Involved"

When Lynn's married daughter moved out of town, Lynn was crushed. She and her daughter had always spent a lot of time together, shopping and cooking and taking Lynn's children to the park. They had a wonderful back-and-forth relationship. Lynn's daughter was her soul-mate.

Lynn's first response after her daughter moved was to feel depressed. For weeks she moped around. Nothing made her happy. She went through the motions of being with others.

"I forced myself to stay involved," she said, "but on the inside I felt hollow."

She swam twice a week, became active in a study group, renewed old friendships. She put one foot in front of the other and kept going.

"I was miserable. I'd go somewhere and couldn't wait to get home," she shared. "Then one day it dawned on me that I hadn't thought of my daughter, not once. My day had been good. I felt content."

Lynn changed gears. She felt lonely and depressed because her daughter had moved away, but she didn't give in to her feelings. She made herself stay involved. She forced herself to pursue various interests. It took about 15 months for her to shake her sadness, but now she's content with life again.

Notice that in discussing Lynn, I said she made herself,

> ***"The misery which follows pleasure is the pleasure which follows misery. The happiness and misery of mankind revolve like a wheel."***
>
> Nagarjuna & Sakya Pandit

she forced herself. Switching gears, changing directions, is not easy, but it's one of the most valuable assets we have as human beings. And it's one of the most important techniques for getting over a hurt or disappointment.

• • •

Think about life as a glass of water with everyone, including yourself, busy swimming around in the glass. Then all of a sudden something happens — your mate leaves, you lose your job — and you're hurled up on top of the glass. Now you're sitting there on the rim looking at all the other people so busy, so involved. You think what they're doing is rather silly, but you also don't like feeling lonely. You don't know what to do or how to get back in the glass. The answer — you try all kinds of things. You learn to play the flute, you start a walking program, you get involved in teaching someone to read, you join a study group. One day you're back in the glass involved in life.

"The only way out is through."
Alcoholics Anonymous Slogan

6

CASE STUDY

"Mostly I'm Brave"

When Frank and Cece danced at their wedding 25 years ago, neither of them could have predicted that by middle age they'd be sitting on the sidelines watching their friends out on the dance floor. After a disc ruptured in Frank's back, affecting his sciatic nerve, he suffered chronic, often debilitating lower back pain.

"It's been a nightmare," says Cece. "We used to go camping and fishing with the children. After Frank's back problem he couldn't pitch a tent, so the boys and I had to do it. He couldn't walk the riverbank. He never said much, but it killed me to watch him. Finally we gave up camping.

"He used to play tennis with the children and basketball in the backyard. That had to end. We used to have friends over for barbecues and parties. We still have friends to our home, but almost all the work is mine. I must do the preparation, the serving and the cleanup. It's exhausting. I know some of our friends don't call us when they get together to go on an outing. Frank would have to sit in the car or on a bench, and that would make them uncomfortable.

"Frank is unable to lift anything and has trouble walking. Standing for even a few minutes is painful. He still works as an accountant, but by evening he's exhausted.

"He comes home and falls asleep watching the news," says Cece. "I try to be supportive, but sometimes I think, 'It's not fair. Frank is a good person. I'm a good person. Why us? Why can't we be on the golf course with our children? Why can't we go apple picking with our family? Why can't we be on the dance floor? I'm young, I want an active life.' Then I think, 'Cut that out. You're not helping yourself or Frank. Stop that thinking.'

"Mostly I'm brave. I count the good things I have. A husband who loves me. Wonderful children. Parents who are healthy. Good friends. Financial security. Faith in God.

"I've started walking by myself in the evening. I think Frank likes that I'm doing this, but I think he's also sad that we can't walk together.

"One thing that pulls me out of feeling sorry for myself is when I think about Frank and his disappointments in life. He's in pain most of the time, yet he never complains. He can't hike or garden. Even waiting in line for the movies is tough. He's had to give up so much. Everyone should meet Frank. They would look at their lives differently."

Frank deals with his disappointment with resignation and quiet acceptance. No complaining, no feeling sorry for himself, no thinking about what life was in the past or could have been in the future. He lives in the present, doing what he can.

Cece struggles more with her disappointment. On some days she accepts Frank's illness and tries to make the best of their life. She mentally reviews what she does have. She says, "I wouldn't trade Frank for anything." On other days she thinks about what she's missing, and she feels sad.

"Be kind, for everyone you meet is fighting a hard battle."

Apples of Gold

Little Bumps Get Us Ready for the Big Ones

Life doesn't provide us with just big hurts; it also gives us plenty of little thumps and bumps along the way. How you deal with these small disappointments is just as important as how you handle the big ones. In fact, I think sometimes the little ones get us ready for the big ones.

For example: the cleaners shrink your favorite suit, a child doesn't care about school and studying, the plumber doesn't come when you've taken off work, a relative makes a hurtful remark, a mate rejects you sexually, the car breaks down, a friend burns a hole in your furniture and says nothing to you, a co-worker doesn't do his fair share. This is part of life. Everyone experiences these bumps. No one escapes. Some months, some years are better. I sometimes think, "This is good. Everything is fine, only a little suffering these last few months."

When pain comes into your life, how do you deal with it? Do you get angry? Cry? Withdraw and feel depressed? Put one foot in front of the other and keep on marching? Focus on something new? Obsess and think, "Why me?" and "It's not fair." Do you look for insight in reading and talking with others? Do you work with a therapist? Do you push the sadness away by refusing to think about it? Do you pray for help?

If you live long enough, you will have pain. No one escapes. How you choose to deal with your pain is what makes the difference.

CHAPTER 7

Are You Aware of How the Werther Effect and the Consistency Principle Influence Your Everyday Life?

As I was growing up, working was always something you just did. Working is part of my response pattern. In my family, you put your feet on the floor in the morning and started. When your workday ended, you went home and cut the grass, worked on the car, painted the fence, repaired the lawnmower, sewed and embroidered, made jelly or planted bulbs you were lucky to get from the neighbors.

> ***"What you hear repeatedly you will eventually believe."***
> Mike Murdock

Every summer my dad and mom took a two-week vacation. We'd drive to Michigan, where my parents' best friends had a farm. The first night my parents and their friends would sit around and talk. We children would play and get reacquainted. The following morning, we were up doing chores. My dad milked cows, combined, repaired machinery and filled the barn with hay. My mom helped feed 15 to 20 farm hands a hot lunch and hot dinner. The women made roasts, hams, fried chicken, fresh vegetables, mashed potatoes and lots of fruit pies. I can still see Mom and her friend Dorothy mashing potatoes in a huge pot on the outside steps.

In addition to all the food preparation, they had seven kids to watch. I was one of them. Since I was the oldest, my job was to keep an eye on the little ones, help peel potatoes, set the table and dry the dishes. Because no one complained about work and everyone did it, I grew up thinking that this is the way you live.

If money was short, as it frequently was, you took an extra job. When I was about seven and had to have my tonsils taken out, my dad took a second job working at the post office during Christmas rush to pay for the operation. When my mother wanted a new kitchen sink, she took a job on Saturday selling chickens.

One of my earliest memories is of standing in a cold garage at night listening to my parents talk and work. It was right after World War II. Dad had come home from the army. He had a day job, but that didn't quite cut the mustard, since my parents were also helping support my grandma and great aunt. At night, to earn extra money, Mom and Dad scraped paint from used cars with a razor blade. They'd take the car down to bare metal. They got paid $25 per car.

> ***"I discovered that the more I hustled, the luckier I seemed to get."***
>
> Fran Tarkenton

Since my husband also came from worker bees (his mother worked a full-time job until she was 76), neither of us knew how to live life differently. I would hear friends say, "Sit down, Doris, relax." I'd say, "I am relaxed." I didn't understand what they meant until one of my clients confronted me.

I was giving him trouble about not getting up and going to work, and he said, "The problem is, you like to work, and I don't." That stopped me in my tracks. Some people don't enjoy working?

Since then, I've gotten a little more balanced in my life. I can honestly say I'm just as happy seeing clients and writing as I am going to the movies and having dinner with friends.

What about you? How do you view work?

- Is work something you dread, like the man who had trouble getting up in the morning?

- Do you see work as a necessary evil — something you have to do, although you would prefer doing something different?

- Do you look forward to putting in the energy and seeing what you can accomplish?

- How does your view of work match your parents' views?

Childhood's Influence

People often think they're not like their parents. But then they hear themselves saying the very same things their parents said. And, on examination, they find that in many ways they are like their parents.

Here's a series of questions designed to help you understand how you've been influenced by your family. Answer the following questions.

1. Was your family happy? Do you consider yourself a happy person?

   ____

   ____

2. When you think about your mom, how are you like her?

   ____

   ____

3. What about your dad? How are you like him?

   ____

   ____

4. What feelings did your mother and father generally express when something didn't go their way? What feelings are you most likely to have when a situation doesn't go your way?

   ____

   ____

5. Did your parents take time for fun, and what did they do? Do you have similar interests?

   ____

   ____

6. What did your parents tell you about education, religion and God? How has this affected your life?

7. Name one thing you do physically with your body — stand with your hands on your hips, tilt your head a certain way, run your hands through your hair — that is identical to the way your mother or father behaved?

8. As a child, if you could have changed anything about each of your parents, what might that have been? Do you have this same issue?

9. How did your parents treat you when you were sick? How do you treat yourself, mate, children when they are ill?

10. What was your parents' view of money? What is your view?

11. Were your parents generous with others? Are you?

12. Were you compared to your siblings or other family members? Do you frequently compare yourself to others?

13. What did your parents tease you about — a habit, a physical characteristic? How do you view that characteristic today?

____

____

14. Did your parents have a favorite motto or saying, and how has this saying affected your life?

____

____

15. Did your parents think you would amount to anything? Have you met their expectations?

____

____

After answering these questions, it's easy to see how you were influenced by your upbringing. It's also interesting to see in what ways you're different from your parents, in what ways you've changed.

Often when people come to therapy, they want to blame their parents for their problems. "I've never done anything with my life because I wasn't encouraged as a child," laments one woman. "I can't make a decision because my parents made all my decisions for me," a man says.

Most definitely your parents had a strong influence on your life. Nevertheless, now you are an adult, and it's your responsibility to change that part of life that you're dissatisfied with. For instance, if you weren't encouraged to study or get an education, OK. Now you can encourage yourself and get an education. Or if you saw your father pout, you, too, may be a pouter. But you don't have to pout. There are more effective ways to show your disapproval. How much you follow what you learned as a child is really up to you.

Having read many research articles on how people are influenced and reading Robert Cialdini's book, *Influence*, I believe that equally as influential as your parents are the people you associate with — your mate, your co-workers, your friends,

> ***"Do the thing you fear, and the death of fear is certain."***
>
> Ralph Waldo Emerson

your neighbors, your church group. In addition, you are strongly influenced by the media — television, radio, movies, books and magazine articles. Many people look at how they were influenced by parents; few examine how their behavior is being influenced by the people they relate to each day.

The Werther Effect and the Principle of Social Proof

In the late 17th century, the German writer Johann von Goethe wrote *The Sorrows of Young Werther*. In the book young Werther shoots himself rather than face life without his true love. Soon after the book's publication, countless young people across Europe committed suicide in emulation of young Werther. In fact, the effect of the book was so powerful that various countries banned its sale.

In the early 1970s, David Phillips, a social psychologist, researched the Werther Effect. Phillips found that after the appearance of a front-page story on suicide, the incidence of suicide significantly increased in the areas where the newspaper was published. Since then, Phillips and other researchers repeatedly have demonstrated through some fascinating experiments that:

1. People decide how to behave based on how others around them are behaving.

2. People are more likely to follow the lead of individuals they view as similar to themselves.

3. When people are unsure of how to act in a given situation, they are especially likely to behave as everyone else does.

4. People decide a behavior is appropriate and correct based on how others around them are behaving.

Let's suppose you start a new job. You're immediately susceptible to behaving like the other people in your department. Their behavior tells you whether to come in early or stay late, how you should dress, how many breaks to take, which jokes are appropriate and how much of your personal life to share.

For example, after working several months with one company, Brad kept hearing from various people about how they padded their expense account. Brad thought this was morally wrong, and he reported only his true expenses. Then one month he had some extra bills, so he decided to turn in a few expenses that he hadn't incurred. Several months later it had become standard operating procedure for him to pad his expense account. He still thought it was wrong, but his behavior had changed. His behavior had been affected by those around him.

> ***"If you have to have a policy manual, publish the 'Ten Commandments.'"***
>
> Robert Townsend, Former CEO Avis

"In this way it was possible to decoy a herd toward a precipice and cause it to plunge over en masse, the leaders being thrust over by their followers, and all the rest following of their own free will, like the sheep who cheerfully leaped, one after another, through a hole in the side of a high bridge because their bellwether did so."[12]

This passage from *"The Extermination of the American Bison"* was written in 1887, referring to a herd of buffalo. It could just as easily be written today referring to individuals who allow themselves to be swept along because "everyone else is doing it."

The Rule of Reciprocation

Another way you may be influenced without knowing it is by the Reciprocation Rule. This unwritten rule says that you should repay in kind what another person has given you. Someone does you a favor, and in return, you should do him or her a favor. It's the old "you scratch my back, I'll scratch yours" philosophy. Sounds reasonable and innocent enough, and it's part of societal expectations, but look at the possible consequences.

> ***"We hire in eagles and teach them to fly in formation."***
>
> D. Wayne Calloway, CEO Pepsi

For example, Joe decides he wants you for a friend. He knows you're interested in tennis, so he invites you to play at his club. You accept. Because of the Reciprocation Rule, you feel obligated to pay Joe back in some way. So you take Joe to a football game. Before you know it, you're socializing with Joe, someone you may or may not want to be friends with.

• • •

Janice is always telling me how much she hates going to lunch with a particular woman. I say, "Why do you keep going when you know you don't have a good time? You don't even like her."

Janice shrugs helplessly and says, "But she keeps calling. She keeps inviting me." Because Janice thinks she is getting something, an invitation, she feels obligated to give back. She gives back by spending time with the woman.

"He who accepts evil without protesting against it is really cooperating with it."

Apples of Gold

• • •

Suppose you're in charge of a department. Everyone knows you love hockey. Someone in the department gives you hockey tickets. You are now indebted. How will you pay this person back? Maybe he'll get a slightly better evaluation. With enough hockey tickets, maybe he'll become the supervisor.

• • •

If you have a child, he or she probably puts the Reciprocation Rule to work every day. Here are some examples. Four-year-old Joannie says, "I gave you a kiss, will you buy me a puzzle?" Ten-year-old Jason says, "Cleaned my room, Mom. Can I go to Marty's house?" And 16-year-old Sherrill says, "Got my homework done. Can I have the car?"

This is the way a lot of businesses get themselves in trouble. They follow the Reciprocation Rule. They give their business to people who in the past have done them a favor, rather than to the company that has the best product. The United States Congress is a good example. Often votes from congressmen are cast not on the basis of the integrity of a bill, but on the basis of a favor.

It's important that a society have unwritten rules and maintain protocol. And reciprocation is part of societal expectations. At the same time, be aware of how this unwritten rule is affecting your life.

The Reciprocal Concession Rule

"Some people can see at a glance what others cannot see with searchlights and telescopes."

Apples of Gold

Another factor that subconsciously influences you is the Reciprocal Concession Rule. This rule says you're obliged to make a concession to someone who's made a concession to you.

For example, you ask your boss if you can take off next Friday. He says, "Fine." He has granted you a concession. He then asks you to work the following weekend. It's your turn to grant him a concession. Seems fair enough. But here, too, you can be unknowingly manipulated.

Suppose your son wants a car. You think he doesn't need a car. Further, buying him a car would place a strain on your family's finances. In talking about a car, your son says, "I'll take a part-time job. I'll pay for the insurance and my gas." With this offer, he's made a concession. Now it's your turn to concede. On Saturday you find yourself looking at cars even though it's not the best thing for your family's financial situation.

Here's another example of the Reciprocal Concession Principle at work.

An engineer says to his boss, "This car's not ready to go into production. It shimmies between 40 and 50 miles an hour."

The supervisor says, "Tell you what. We'll slide the schedule. We'll delay production six months, and you work things out."

What's happened? The boss has granted a concession — a delay. Now it's the engineer's turn to grant a concession. Six months later he signs off on the car even though it still shimmies.

That's how defective products often get on the market. Everyone is granting concessions.

This week watch for those who are willing to grant you a concession. Then see if you grant one back. Additionally, check to see if the concession you granted is really in everyone's best interest.

7

The Consistency Principle

Another rule that continually influences you is the Consistency Principle.

Within each person is a desire to appear or act consistent. It is part of everyone's response pattern. Once you've made a decision, you tend to hold to that decision.

I have a friend who's very overweight. He tells me he's never been thin. His view of himself is that he's fat. He tells me he has always been fat, and he'll always be fat.

I convinced him to go on a low-fat diet a few years ago. I even prepared a few meals to show him how tasty they could be. He immediately lost weight. But then he went back to his old ways of eating, and his weight went right back up. As long as his view of himself is that he's fat, he'll stay that way. He has bought into the Consistency Principle.

• • •

A boss promotes someone, but within weeks it's clear that he's made the wrong choice. Instead of moving the person to a different position, however, the boss holds to his original decision. Within him is an overwhelming desire to see himself as consistent, as well as to have others view him as consistent.

• • •

You go to buy a new car. Before buying it you're all in a stew, wondering if you should spend the money and if you're making the best selection. As you drive out of the dealer's lot, one hour later, you're telling yourself what a smart, good decision you've made. It's not that you have any more information about the car than you did an hour earlier; it's just that you are powerfully motivated to believe you made a good decision. The Consistency Principle has taken effect.

• • •

"There is no pillow as soft as a clear conscience."

The Power of Ethical Management

Ralph came to see me for therapy because he had a nasty temper, and his company told him to learn to cool it. When we first talked, he told me he'd always had problems with his anger. "In fact, my whole family is a bunch of hotheads," he confessed.

One of the things I did was have him say, "I choose not to be angry, I choose to be in control" 3,000 times a day. In addition, he had to call my office every day for a month and tell me he was saying the sentence and staying in control. If he missed a day, and he missed plenty in the beginning, he had to start the 30-day period over.

The reason for the assignment of 30 days in a row was that I wanted him to start viewing himself as a person who could do what he set out to do. He could control his anger. He's now one of my biggest fans.

Many things influence you. Your parents, grandparents, teachers, a sermon, a book, the way people around you behave, television, movies. In understanding yourself, it's most important to know how you are being influenced, and whether or not you want that particular way of thinking, feeling and behaving to be part of your life.

Random Acts of Kindness

There's a movement afoot that suggests we can make this world a better place by doing random acts of kindness. For example, give up your seat on the subway. Let someone go in front of you in a checkout line. Carry someone's grocery bag. Hold open the door for a group of people. Buy movie tickets and give them away.

If this movement really catches on, it will be because of: (1) the Werther Effect — people decide how to behave based on how others around them are behaving; (2) the Consistency Principle — if you view yourself as a good person, you will behave like a good person; (3) the Reciprocation Rule — as you do kind acts for others, they in turn will do kind acts. And soon, there will be acts of kindness everywhere.

> ***"Happiness is a perfume you cannot pour on others without getting a few drops on yourself."***
>
> Apples of Gold

• • •

A story is told of two birds sitting on the limb of a tree, quietly watching the snow as it fell ever so lightly. The young bird looked over at his companion and said, "How much does a snowflake weigh?" The older bird said, "Why, it weighs nothing more than nothing."

The snow continued to fall, and after some time the older bird flew away. The younger bird decided that he would count the snowflakes that fell on the limb below. He counted thousands and tens of thousands, and soon he came to the number 3,700,001. He then counted 3,700,002. At that point the branch broke.[13]

If one snowflake that weighs "Nothing more than nothing" can make a difference, think of the difference a parent, husband, friend, teacher, salesman, musician, engineer, secretary can make. Think of the difference you can make.

CHAPTER 8

Do You Allow Yourself the Feeling of Intimacy?

8

"Independence? That's middle-class blasphemy. We are all dependent on one another, every soul of us on earth."

George Bernard Shaw

When my dad was growing up, no one taught him to say, "I love you." It wasn't what people, particularly men, said 75 years ago.

Through the years I would put my arms around my dad and say, "I love you, Dad."

He'd pat me on the back and say, "That's nice."

I'd smile and say, "Dad, say 'I love you' back to me."

He'd hem and haw and say, "You know I love you."

I'd say, "Yes, I know. But I want you to tell me."

Finally after years of nudging, my dad has come around, and whenever he is leaving our house or ending a conversation on the telephone, he says, "I love you."

Recently, Dad's become hard-of-hearing. This past spring he was helping me put in some new rose bushes, and I said something to him about mulching them. He looked at me, smiled, and said, "I love you, too."

What a wonderful moment of intimacy.

Many people have the idea that intimacy happens only over candlelight dinners or on sandy beaches in the Caribbean. Certainly these places can set the stage for intimacy. But intimacy is just as likely to happen in a shopping mall, in the lunch room at work or among strangers cheering wildly at the Super Bowl.

Intimacy. You often hear the word, but what is it?

Intimacy is that feeling of connectedness and closeness that bonds, for a moment in time, one human being to another, to a group, to God, to nature, to the world.

Intimacy can be one-way — I can feel intimate with you without you having any knowledge of my feelings.

Intimacy can happen simultaneously between two people. I feel intimate with you, and you feel intimate with me.

Intimacy can be experienced in a crowd of strangers. I feel intimate with all these people who are jumping up and down and cheering because our home team just scored a basket.

Intimacy can be experienced as you watch the sunset or stand by a roaring stream. And sometimes that feeling of closeness and connectedness almost knocks you down, and you feel intimate with God.

So often I see the words "intimacy" and "love" used interchangeably, but intimacy and love are not the same. Intimacy is not love. Love is not intimacy. Intimacy is a feeling. Love is action.

One-Way Intimacy

Here are some examples of one-way intimacy.

I stand at the window watching my daughter determinedly trudge up an icy hill with her sled. I feel a connectedness, a closeness with her. I experience one-way intimacy.

I listen to my husband singing "Rain Drops Keep Falling on My Head" in the shower. I smile and feel connected.

Yesterday a hummingbird was caught under the roof of my front porch. I got a dust mop, put it under him, and very slowly edged him up to the roof line. When there was nowhere else for him to go, he settled into the mop. I then took the mop out from under the porch and held it up in the air. After a few seconds he realized he had his freedom and off he hummed. As he left the dust mop, I felt a moment of intimacy with that tiny bird.

"Happiness is someone to love and something to look forward to."

Anonymous

You're shopping and notice a mother kissing her little boy all over while he giggles and wiggles in her arms. You experience a feeling of connectedness to both the mother and child.

You're standing on a mountain ready to ski down, and you become overwhelmed with a feeling of oneness, of intimacy with nature.

You pick up the telephone, and it's your son calling. You're happy, pleased, excited, connected, intimate.

A woman told me she feels intimate when she looks at her husband and his hair is all rumpled. "He's a banker and almost always looks impeccable," she says. "His rumpled hair turns him into a little boy."

Some people say they experience one-way intimacy many times a day. A question to ask yourself: ***How often do I allow myself to feel this type of intimacy?***

If your answer is "not enough," take the time to look, to see. Give yourself the present of intimacy.

Two-Way Intimacy

Two-way intimacy happens when both people experience that feeling of connectedness and closeness at the same moment in time.

You and your husband are in the delivery room. The doctor says, "Well, this time you've got yourselves a little girl." You look at each other and experience intimacy.

The other day I was eating a hot fudge sundae. All of a sudden my friend noticed I had chocolate all over my clothes — on my coat sleeve, my blouse, and my blue jeans. We started howling with laughter. We felt intimate.

You're fishing with a friend. He gets a strike. He flashes you a smile and says, "Did you see that?" You nod and briefly the two of you experience intimacy.

I was having a cup of coffee on the second floor of a shopping mall, watching all the shoppers below. I saw a couple,

"Put your ass in the ball, Mr. President."

Sam Snead, progolfer, to Dwight D. Eisenhower

who probably were in their seventies, standing by one of the fountains. They both were wearing navy blue berets. Suddenly they looked up and saw me looking at them. I waved, pointed to their berets, smiled, and nodded my head in approval. They smiled and each of them blew me a kiss. I blew two kisses back. Intimacy in progress.

> ***"What sunshine is to flowers, smiles are to humanity."***
>
> Apples of Gold

Intimacy in a Crowd

If you've ever been to a sporting event, you've probably experienced intimacy with a lot of other people. Your team scores a touchdown, and everyone starts jumping up and down, hugging and laughing. You experience, for that moment in time, a feeling of connectedness to all the other people who are jumping up and down. Then the moment is over. You get quiet. You sit down in your seat. And the intimacy is gone.

I believe this is one reason so many people enjoy sporting events. It's a place to experience emotional intimacy.

Thwarting Intimacy

So often we have a chance at intimacy and we muff it.

For example, we were on vacation with friends. The husband was reading the newspaper at the kitchen table. The wife, who had just gotten up, walked into the kitchen. On seeing his wife, the guy said, "What are you doing up so early?"

Ugh! How was this wife supposed to respond?

Had this man looked up, smiled at his wife, and said, "Hi, honey," they might have enjoyed a moment of closeness.

Here are two other moments of lost intimacy:

Peggy was shopping at the mall and decided to buy some candy. As she approached the candy counter, she saw an acquaintance of hers. She smiled and asked the man, "What are you buying?"

He looked at her and said, "Candy."

Immediately Peggy was put off. He had implied she was a dummy. Too bad the man didn't tell her what kind of candy he was choosing. Then the two of them might have shared their likes and dislikes.

• • •

Stan was grilling hamburgers. All of a sudden he had a brainstorm. He turned to his wife and said, "Let's eat out here on the porch. It's such a great night."

His wife's response, "No, it's too buggy."

Perhaps if this woman had thought one second longer before she responded, she wouldn't have rained on her husband's parade.

Often a person will make a suggestion to do something and almost before it's out of his mouth, someone else will nix it. Once you say no, even if you later reconsider and say yes, you've missed a chance for intimacy.

> ***"I have observed that folks are generally as happy as they have made up their minds to be."***
>
> Apples of Gold

• • •

Criticism and anger are the two biggest ways to thwart intimacy. If you are thinking a negative thought or feeling angry, intimacy will not happen. You cannot hate and feel close at the same time. In addition, once you've been critical or angry with someone, it's going to take time before the other person lets down his guard, trusts you again, and opens himself up for the possibility of intimacy.

Being too busy also keeps you from feeling intimate. If you don't take time to listen to your inner feelings, observe what's going on around you, and interact with others, intimacy won't happen.

Setting the Stage for Intimacy

> ***"Plant trees where you will never sit."***
>
> Anonymous

I don't think you can make intimacy happen, but you certainly can be open to it.

As I write this book, I've been watching the hummingbirds at the feeder. Now, I can't make them come to my house, but

I can set the stage. I can have a feeder always filled with food and plant their favorite flowers in my garden. I can make it inviting for those little fellows to come around.

Here are some ways to set the stage for intimacy:

- Watch a funny movie with your family. Each time you all laugh, there's a possibility that one of you will look at the other and you'll feel that special closeness.
- Listen respectfully and quietly as someone talks.
- Look through an old family photo album.
- Take a walk with a friend.
- Stop by a church for a quiet visit.
- Tell a joke to a co-worker.
- Bring everyone at the office a rose.
- Confide a dream for the future.
- Look up and smile broadly when someone comes in the room.
- Sit quietly in a lawn chair.
- Take a drive in the country.
- Invite friends over for a chili dinner.
- Notice how your pet greets you when you come home.
- Give someone a compliment, a present, a hug.

The more you open yourself up to intimacy, the more it will come to you. It's available. It's plentiful. It's free. It makes you feel loved and loving. It's energizing and calming. It's miraculous. It's awesome. You can have it 50 times a day if you like.

What more could any human being ask for?

CHAPTER 9

Are You a Faultfinding, Critical Person?

9

For holidays and birthdays a group of us routinely get together to celebrate. We talk, laugh, tell jokes, ride horses, and solve world problems. These celebrations always include a sit-down dinner. After dinner we play a funny little game. We've been doing it for years.

Someone moves his or her plate and glass and announces, "Look how clean my place is."

Not to be outdone, others at the table move their dishes and inspect the tablecloth in front of them. When a spill is spotted, everyone hoots and hollers.

One particular gentleman almost always is declared the messiest. We tease him unmercifully about his spatters and spills, and he laughs good-naturedly.

At our last gathering this very gentleman started the game. He said, "Look at me. Look at my place. Not a single spill. I win."

We all carefully compared his place to ours, and, sure enough, we declared him the winner. As we sat cheering and toasting him, his wife said, "Now, if you could only do that at home."

This was a critical comment.

Did this man's wife intend to be critical of her husband at the moment of his triumph? Was her comment a ploy to shift the attention away from her husband and onto herself? What was she thinking and feeling? What drove her remark?

Unfortunately, this woman is not alone in her behavior.

> ***"One reason why a dog is such a lovable creature is that his tail wags instead of his tongue."***
>
> Apples of Gold

Wives and husbands freely make critical comments to each other. Many parents criticize their children 20 or 30 times a day. Co-workers and bosses fire off disparaging remarks. Friends take potshots and laugh, or they try to hide their criticisms under the guise of helpful suggestions.

I wonder: Is there no safe haven from criticism? Why are so many people critical? Don't people understand how criticism affects others?

In the following stories you will meet a number of critical people. As you read, ask yourself: ***Am I like this person?***

Every year the Baker family — mom, dad, three grown daughters and a grown son — go to Aunt Marie's house to help her with spring cleaning. This is the family's gift to Aunt Marie.

This year one of the things the family did was drag out the patio furniture and wash it. Afterwards, as everyone was sitting around admiring their efforts, Mom said, "Look at that dirt at the bottom of that chair. I bet it's the one your father washed."

No one made a comment. But eyes rolled knowingly, as if to say, "Here she goes again."

Later in the day one of the daughters realized that her dad had been out in the heat too long trimming bushes. So the daughter went to the door and called out, "Dad, come on in and take a rest. You're working too hard." Before her dad had a chance to respond, Mom piped up and said, "He won't come in. You know your father. He's afraid he'll miss something."

Toward evening, as the family gathered at the table and everyone was filling their plates, Mom took yet another swipe at Dad. This time she said, "Well, are you going to pass those pork chops, dear, or are you going to hog them all for yourself?"

What this woman fails to comprehend is that her negative comments are a turnoff. Mom is certainly doing a good deed, helping her sister. But she loses her family's love and respect because of her critical comments. What she doesn't understand is that the children do not want to hear their father being put down.

• • •

"You will always move toward anyone who increases you and away from anyone who makes you less."

Mike Murdock

As you read the next story, you'll see how Ralph inadvertently made Janet's evening miserable. It all started when Janet asked Ralph to go to the movies.

"Ralph," said Janet, "let's go to a movie tonight."

Ralph's response: "That doesn't sound good to me."

Disappointed, Janet said, "Well, I think I'll go anyway." As she was getting her things together, Ralph suddenly clicked off the television and announced he would be joining her.

Janet, who had already switched plans in her head, asked, "Are you sure you want to go?"

Ralph assured her he did.

As they drove into the theater parking lot, Ralph mumbled that the last movie must not have let out yet. So where did they expect everybody to park? Certainly the theater could do a better job of scheduling.

As they waited in line to buy tickets, Ralph said that everybody and their brother must have decided to see this movie, judging by the length of the line. Janet, sensing Ralph's annoyance, made small talk, hoping to divert him from making any more critical observations.

When they got into the lobby, Janet suggested Ralph get seats, and she would get the popcorn.

Ralph said, "You're going to stand in that line just for popcorn?" Janet nodded.

With her popcorn in hand, Janet made her way to where Ralph was seated. His comment on seeing her: "You didn't get anything to drink?"

"No," she said. But she offered to go back to get him a drink.

"Never mind," said Ralph.

"Really, I'll go back," Janet said. "I just didn't think you'd want anything."

"I don't now," said Ralph. As they sat in silence waiting for the show to start, Janet struggled with feelings of guilt over the drink and irritation over Ralph's negativism.

Once Ralph commented that the popcorn tasted stale.

At the end of the movie Janet asked, "What did you think?"

Ralph shrugged and said, "It was OK."

They drove home in silence.

CASE STUDY

9

"Faults are thick when love is thin."

Apples of Gold

Are You a Faultfinder?

Critical people are always finding fault with someone or something. They simply can't resist pointing out the problem. With critical people nothing is good enough, right enough. If you go out to dinner with someone who is critical, the food is overcooked or undercooked. The restaurant is too expensive, or the service is poor. If you listen to a critical person talk politics, you'd swear the country was going to hell in a handbasket. To be in an automobile with a critical person is torture. Nobody on the road knows how to drive. When critical people read the newspaper, listen to the news or watch television, what is wrong with the world becomes the focus of their attention.

> ***"Try to fix the mistake — never the blame."***
>
> Apples of Gold

Faultfinders tend to have other characteristics in common. Almost always they expect perfection of themselves as well as others. Rarely are they satisfied. Their internal dialogue is often about what hasn't been done and what needs to get done. They are driven by a lot of oughts and shoulds.

Some of their favorite phrases include, "You should do this," "You need to do that," "Why don't you," "How come you don't," and "I think you should." I've also noticed that they do a lot of wagging of their pointer finger to get their message across. In therapy I'm always saying, "Stop wagging your pointer."

Most people who are critical and judgmental are also determined people. They are responsible. They can be counted on. If they say they will do something, chances are they will do it.

Criticism Backfires — Almost Always

Making critical comments will not help you win friends or influence people. Just the contrary. Criticism almost always derails relationships and drives people away.

For example, I've had a number of women come to me for therapy in order to get help dealing with their critical mothers. Their comments all have a familiar ring.

"My mother tells me she's lonely and has no friends. At the same time all she does is criticize her friends. Nothing they do is right."

"My mom is always complaining about my dad. I know he's difficult to live with, but I don't want to keep hearing about it."

"Mom never has anything nice to say about anyone. All she does is complain. I can hardly stand to be around her."

If you've noticed your grown child avoiding you, take inventory, listen to yourself.

"Before you flare up at anyone's faults, take time to count ten — ten of your own."

Apples of Gold

• • •

Another thing to keep in mind: Criticism does not get people to change, even if your criticism is valid.

Countless men have complained to me in therapy about their critical wives. Clearly these men have flaws that need to be addressed, and in many ways they actually invite their wives to lecture them because of their discounting behavior. However, I have not seen a man change his behavior because of a lecture. If anything, he's more apt to dig in his heels and resist making any change.

For example, your husband is forever coming home late. You've asked him repeatedly to please call if he's going to be late. He says he will, but he never does. You confront, you criticize, you lecture. Does he change? No.

A child continually brings home poor grades. The parent's response — constant badgering. "If you would only study. Can't you see how you're ruining your life?" Does this criticism bring in better grades? No. But it does create a home filled with tension and resentment.

• • •

I'm seeing a man in therapy who has cheated on his wife. His wife is in a rage. At this point they are separated. Every time they get together to see if they can work things out, she lets him have it. Her criticisms and anger are certainly valid and understandable, but they won't help her save the marriage.

• • •

If you're a critical person, people will not trust you because they know that, sooner or later, they, too, will fall prey to your criticism. People will put their guard up and eventually all spontaneity will disappear as they must carefully choose their words and watch their actions. Over time, they won't even want to be with you.

Manipulating with Criticism

It's interesting that some people use criticism as a ploy to try to get closer to someone. For example, every time I meet this one man at a party, he seems compelled to tell me some negative story about his wife. Perhaps he thinks these tales bring us closer, sort of like the two of us against her. In reality his behavior causes me to avoid him.

Some individuals are so insecure with themselves, and so competitive, that they use critical observations to put others down in order to make themselves look better. Trying to make yourself look better by devaluing someone else never works, however, because people always see through your tactics. You may not think they do, but they do.

> ***"Creativity is a flower that praise brings to bloom, but discouragement often nips in the bud."***
>
> Alex F. Osborn

• • •

Another tactic critical people use: They give a compliment and then negate it with a critical remark.

A friend who is an accomplished musician was taking a saxophone lesson. After he finished playing a particularly difficult piece, his teacher said, "You played that rather well. I'm amazed." My friend said he felt terrible and wished the teacher had made no comment at all.

• • •

A grandmother took her granddaughter shopping. When they got home, the grandmother said to her grown daughter, "What a nice time we had." Then she added, "But your daughter sure doesn't understand the value of a dollar."

This comment criticized not only the granddaughter, but the daughter as well. Again, why make such a comment? What purpose does it serve? People who make critical comments would do well to ask themselves the question that Luke posed:

"Why do you observe the splinter in your brother's eye and never notice the great log in your own?" [14]

Luke 6:41

You Can Be Critical Without Opening Your Mouth

I'm always amazed how adept couples in therapy are at criticizing each other without saying a word. Their mouths fly open, they thrust their heads back and their chins forward, they dramatically raise their eyebrows, they cross their arms across their chest. The messages they're sending with these actions: you're stupid, you're a liar, you don't know what you're talking about.

"It is not enough to be busy — the question is: What are we busy about?"

Henry David Thoreau

When I see this kind of nonverbal behavior, I immediately say, "Stop that. If you disagree, say so, but do it appropriately." At the beginning of someone's therapy, I may confront that person 20 times in one session for his negative nonverbals.

Right now take a moment and think about what you do with your body to indicate disapproval. I, myself, put my hands on my hips, squint my eyes, purse my lips, and stick out my chin like a disagreeable four-year-old. I must look ridiculous.

How Did You Become a Negative Person?

> ***"To speak kindly does not hurt the tongue."***
>
> Apples of Gold

Many roads lead to negativity. Sometimes a person is born into a family in which one or both parents are critical. As a result the child grows up learning to look at the world from a negative perspective.

People sometimes become critical because their fantasy of how life was going to be does not match up with reality. Their husband isn't as attentive as they had imagined. They don't have the life-style they planned to have. Their children are not as loving as they had envisioned.

People may become bitter because life has been hard on them. They are married to a selfish mate, they've had terrible financial problems, they've had to deal with a chronic illness or one failed project after another. They become consumed by the event. They can't seem to get beyond it.

People also can become faultfinders if they live or work with negative people. If someone around you is always pointing out mistakes, flaws and injustices, it's easy to start focusing on mistakes, flaws and injustices in life.

Is It Ever Appropriate to Be Critical?

Sometimes people ask — Is it ever appropriate to be critical? Yes, it's expected that a parent correct a child who is misbehaving. Sometimes it's appropriate for an employer to tell a worker when he's not performing. And sometimes it's necessary for a therapist, teacher, minister or friend to confront a person on his or her destructive behavior. Any time an evaluation is required or requested, there is a chance that someone is going to be criticized. At the same time, if criticism is driven by anger or jealousy or competitiveness, or is intended to be manipulative, it's inappropriate.

Wake Up and Become Less Critical

> *"Make up your mind you can't — and you're always right."*
>
> Bob Goddard

If you know you're too critical, decide to change. Write down for one week every disparaging comment you make.

I used this technique with a mother and her 24-year-old daughter who had to move back home because of financial problems. Both mother and daughter knew how critical each could be. And they were concerned that living together wasn't going to work because of their inclination to criticize.

Here are some of the criticisms the mother had, but fortunately did not verbalize:

- Don't you brush your teeth first thing in the morning?
- Are you going to wear that shirt again without washing it?
- Would you please get your car fixed before your engine blows up?
- Isn't that the fourth shower you've taken today?
- There's a button missing on that blouse.
- Do you have your glasses?
- Stop watching television and go do something constructive.
- Your room is starting to look like a pig pen. Where is your pride?
- Don't forget to call your friend back.

> *"One of the best things a man can have up his sleeve is a funny-bone."*
>
> Apples of Gold

And now the daughter's list of complaints:

- Those shoes look ridiculous.
- Why are you wearing nylons with shorts and sandals? If you could just see yourself.

- Can't you drive a little faster?
- Get those curlers out of your hair!
- Don't you ever shave your legs?
- Are you going to stand there and listen to my entire conversation?
- Are you going to wear that? It has got to be 100 years old.
- Why don't you just chill out, relax, calm down.

Less than a week had gone by when the two of them decided to share their list. Although this was not part of the therapy plan, both of them had a good laugh when they read what they had written about each other. It seemed that the mother had a preoccupation with cleanliness, and the daughter was preoccupied with Mom's appearance.

"No echoes return to mock the silent tongue."

Apples of Gold

After going over each other's list, mother and daughter decided that they definitely needed to keep their criticisms to themselves.

Writing down your critical comments is work, but it makes you accountable. And if you truly want to become a less critical person, this method will get you there. Also, writing down your grievances will help you dissipate some of the negative feelings you've generated by your critical thoughts.

Old Fable

There is an old Eastern European fable —

The wind and the sun were having an argument about who was the most powerful. So they decided to have a contest.

The wind said to the sun, "See that man with the coat walking on the sidewalk down below. I bet I can get him to give up his coat, whereas you could never exert such power."

The sun agreed to the challenge.

The wind started whistling and howling and blowing harder and harder. Shutters banged. Shingles flew off houses. People were frightened and hid under their beds. No one had seen such a gale.

But the harder the wind blew, the more the man pulled his coat tightly around him. Finally breathless, the wind died down.

The sun said, "Now I shall have a turn." At that moment the sun started shining brighter and brighter. Now it was dancing brilliantly across the sky. Down below the man relaxed his grip on his coat and no longer held it tightly to his body.

Soon the man could be seen rolling up his coat sleeves.

Soon he took off his coat.

Say It Three Thousand Times a Day

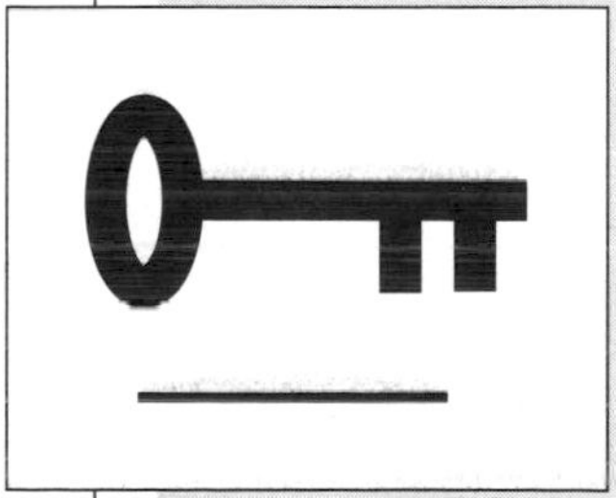

Another technique I use: When someone comes into therapy and admits they're too critical, I have them say 3,000 times a day, ***"I choose not to be critical, but quiet."*** If you are a critical person, say this statement to yourself a few times just to get the feel of its power. ***"I choose not to be critical, but quiet."***

After doing this assignment, many people have said, "It's working. I'm not being critical."

It takes longer than a week to change faultfinding behavior, but with vigilance and continual use of this affirmation, you'll get there. Or as Benjamin Franklin quipped, ***"Each year one vicious habit rooted out, in time might make the worse man (or woman) good throughout."***[15]

I Confess

> ***"Dreams come true when you pay the price."***
>
> Nido R. Qubein

Because I've struggled to be quiet instead of saying something critical, I'd like to share the following story with you.

It was Easter Sunday. We were in the car on our way to our friends' farm. As we were driving along, my husband said, "Easter just doesn't seem like that big of a deal anymore."

What I immediately wanted to say was, "I can't believe you. You may not think it's a big deal, but I made a sweet potato casserole, I got the wine, I bought a gift for our friends, I made an Easter basket for my parents. I stayed up until midnight helping Anna-Mary make two lamb cakes. And I packed the car before church this morning."

Instead I was silent. I was quiet. I said nothing.

As we drove, I started to think. I guess for my husband, Easter probably isn't that big a deal since our children are older. He no longer has to hide Easter eggs at the crack of dawn. There are no little wagons or wheelbarrows to put together. No tiny children to chase around and get dressed for church.

If I had chosen to run out my litany of everything I had done in preparation for Easter, my husband would surely have felt attacked. After the attack, I would have felt guilty and then remorseful. And I would have spoiled a nice ride to the farm.

That night, as we were driving home, my husband reached over, took my hand and said, "It was sure nice, all the things you did for everyone."

CHAPTER 10

How Jealous and Competitive Are You?

Imagine saying to someone, "I don't like you because you're prettier than I am, or a better athlete, or smarter, or taller, or better off financially." Or, "I don't like you because you have the bigger office, or drive a better car, or your children are so successful. I only like you when you do less well than me." But that's the way you think when you're jealous.

"Our purpose in life is not to get ahead of other people, but to get ahead of ourselves."

Nathaniel Emmons

People who suffer from jealousy constantly compare themselves to others. They are always assessing, measuring and evaluating. If in their judgment they win the competition, they feel happy and sometimes a bit smug. If they lose the competition, they feel disappointed and annoyed.

Is this you? Do you constantly compare, evaluate and feel badly when someone else wins the competition you have set up in your head?

CASE STUDY

The Jealous Woman

Colleen's jealousy ruined what could have been a wonderful day. Colleen and her husband had just put a down payment on a house. The day before, she had learned they were going to have a baby boy. Colleen was ecstatic. Life

> *"No person will make a great business who wants to do it all himself or get all the credit."*
>
> Andrew Carnegie

CASE STUDY

couldn't get any better, she thought. Then she ran into her friend Marge. Marge, too, was feeling happy. She had been promoted to one of the television networks and would be moving to New York. Luckily her boyfriend had been able to find a job with a good firm in the city.

When Colleen left Marge, she didn't feel as content and happy as she had before. She wanted to continue to feel good, but she couldn't.

That night with her husband, she was more quiet than usual. When he asked what was wrong, she said, "Nothing. I'm just tired."

Colleen knew, but was too embarrassed to admit, that she was feeling envious, jealous, competitive with Marge. Colleen knew also that she didn't want her friend's life. She wanted to be married and have this child. She understood that she was allowing the news of her friend's good fortune to cause her to feel down and to ruin a potentially fine evening with her husband.

• • •

Because jealousy is a flaw that most people have difficulty acknowledging in themselves, I asked some people to talk about their jealous feelings:

"When we are with our friends, I'm always comparing myself to other women," said Louise. "If I think someone looks better than I look, I can't have a good time. I try, but my evening is a little ruined."

"My business is pretty cutthroat," said a stockbroker. "When a guy tells me he's had a bad day, I find myself feeling a little happy. Stupid, huh?"

"I have a good job," explained Kim, "lots of contacts. Because of this, people are always asking me to do them a favor, use my influence to get them an interview with the company. I tell them OK, sure, but then I don't do it. I worked hard to get where I am. The way I figure it, why should I help someone else? I'm not saying I'm proud of myself for feeling this way, but no one made it easy for me."

"Our son and daughter have done very well. They both have nice homes, nicer than ours. They take expensive trips. I'm glad for them. But sometimes I'm envious. We provided them with their education, paid for all of it, and now they live better than we do.

You're not going to use my name, are you?"

"I can be driving in my car, feeling quite peaceful and listening to the radio," said Sandra, "when I hear that someone else has been honored with an award. All of a sudden I don't feel good. I start ruminating about why I haven't been honored. My whole mood changes."

In the 18th century, Moshe Luzzatto had great insight on envy when he wrote:

"Envy, too, is nothing but want of reason and foolishness, for the one who envies gains nothing for himself and deprives the one he envies of nothing. ... There are those who are so foolish that if they perceive their neighbor to possess a certain good, they brood and worry and suffer to the point that their neighbor's good prevents them from enjoying their own."[16]

Behaviors That Reveal Jealousy

Often people think they are hiding their jealous feelings, yet every day their behavior indicates jealousy. For example, you feel jealous of how much money a friend makes, so you talk about how little time he gives to his family. You feel envious of a co-worker's good looks, so you make disparaging comments about how she cheated on her first husband. When I meet people who are always talking against others, I wonder if their motivation is jealousy.

"Don't carry a grudge. While you're carrying the grudge the other guy's out dancing."
Buddy Hackett

Holding back and not applauding someone else's achievements is another way jealousy raises its ugly head.

I still remember when I got my first book contract. I called a fellow writer I had admired and praised many times through the years. When I told him about the contract and the publisher, he said, "They're a bad publisher."

My stomach knotted and I felt terrible. I wanted so much for him to share in my happiness. Our relationship worked when *he* got the attention, but it didn't work so well when I expected it.

Our friendship waned after this incident. He probably felt competitive and didn't want to see me, and I felt uncared for. Then a year later we ran into each other on the street, and he apologized. He said he was struggling with his writing and had felt jealous when I told him of my good fortune.

Why a Jealous Response?

If you suffer from jealousy, look inside yourself for the reason why. The answer is there.

If as a child you were always compared unfavorably to a sibling or a classmate, chances are you operate from a competitive frame of reference. This means you continually measure yourself against others. If you fall short in any way, your response is to feel jealous.

It may be that you received far more attention than most as a child. As an adult you continue to have the same expectations. Why wouldn't you?

> ***"Be careful how you live; you will be the only Bible some people ever read."***
>
> Anonymous

I'm working with a woman in therapy who rarely feels she gets enough attention. She's always comparing what her husband does for her versus what her friends' husbands do for them. At her job she compares how much praise her boss gives her versus how much praise he gives others in the department. She was an only child and an only grandchild. She admits, "The world revolved around me." Now when she doesn't have the attention, she feels envious of whoever is getting it. Today her struggle is to put a halt to her constant comparing and to learn to be satisfied with less attention.

Sometimes jealousy arises from never feeling secure within yourself. Perhaps you could never accept yourself because your parents never accepted themselves. Maybe they were embarrassed about their educational level, the house they lived in or the fact that they were the least successful of their brothers and sisters. This feeling of insecurity and continual comparing was quietly passed from them to you.

Perhaps a series of incidents in school helped set the stage for you to feel insecure — you had few friends, you were a poor athlete or you had a body type that our society does not see as attractive.

Maybe your self-doubt started as an adult. You were not able to accomplish what you had hoped, your children haven't turned out as you expected, your partner is not emotionally supportive. Now you look around and feel envious of those whose life seems more desirable.

How to Quell the Green-Eyed Monster

To end jealous feelings, you must stop operating from a competitive frame of reference. Do not allow yourself to compare. If someone tells you they just got a great job offer, keep your thoughts focused on the other person. Ask them questions about the new job. Think about how hard they work. Keep yourself out of the equation. If you don't compare, you won't be able to feed your jealousy.

Another technique: Appeal to your reason. Tell yourself over and over: Every time I compare myself to someone else, one of us wins and one of us loses. Do I really want to set myself up to have bad feelings? Also ask yourself, "Why shouldn't he reap what he has sown?"

A third suggestion: Think about what would make you more secure within yourself. Becoming proficient at the piano? Getting more education? Losing weight? Instead of focusing on what others have, focus on what you can do to feel more positive about yourself. When someone suffers from jealousy, I ask the person to write down 10 things each day she likes about herself and read over the list a few times during the day. This exercise helps you to focus on your attributes and stops you from thinking competitively.

"There is something that is much more scarce, something rarer than ability. It is the ability to recognize ability."

Robert Half

Another goal is to think about what achievement or success you envy in another. Then ask yourself, "Am I willing to put in the time and energy it took that person to reach her goal?" For example, you may be jealous of the way your friend plays tennis. Are you willing to put in as many hours taking lessons and practicing?

Another question to ask: "Would I really trade my life for his life, knowing I must accept his disappointments, sufferings and flaws along with what I desire?"

Sometimes jealousy will grab you when you least expect it. For example, someone tells you they just received a large inheritance. Instantly you think competitive thoughts and feel jealous. Instead of displaying your jealousy, make an appropriate comment such as, "That's great." If a couple says their son was accepted to Harvard, congratulate them. You may feel jealous, but you don't have to act on this feeling. You don't have to behave in a competitive manner.

Grabbing Center Stage

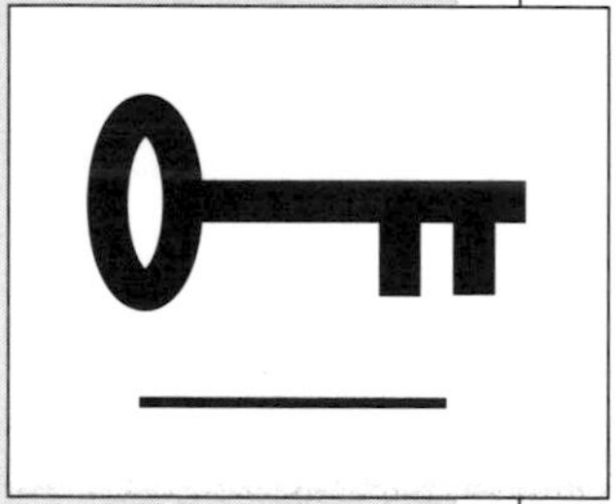

Similar to people who act jealous are people who compete with others for attention. Sometimes the root cause of this competition is jealousy. Sometimes it's insecurity. Sometimes it's a result of always expecting to be center stage.

People who talk too much are attention competitive. As long as they keep talking, they have the attention. What they convey by their constant prattle is "Recognize me. Pay attention to me."

Are you guilty of talking too much?

> ***"Character is what you have when nobody is looking."***
>
> Marie Dresslar

• • •

Interrupting is another competitive behavior. Someone is telling a story, and you butt in and take over. You may continue the story or tell an entirely different one.

Another way of competing is to start a side conversation.

A person is talking, and you start a conversation with someone else. This is a maneuver to take some of the attention away from the person who has the floor.

Every time you interrupt or start a side conversation, you're covertly saying, "Pay attention to me. What I have to say is more important than what others have to say. I count more."

Think. ***How many times have you interrupted someone today? How many side conversations have you started?***

• • •

Attention-competitive people do not listen. When someone else is talking, they allow their minds to wander. They may think of a call they want to make or an item they want to pick up from the store. Also, as the other person is talking, they rarely ask questions or make a comment.

Do you pretend to listen while not listening at all? Is someone always saying to you, "Don't you remember? I told you that yesterday."

• • •

Acting unenthusiastic or unappreciative is another subtle form of keeping the attention on yourself. A friend gives you a sweater, and you don't even take it out of the box. You say, "Oh, that's nice," close the box, and say nothing more.

Here are some additional examples of shifting the attention away from another and onto yourself.

A woman says to her husband, "I think I'm coming down with a cold." His response: "Oh no, now I'll get it." Notice how rapidly the husband diverts the attention away from his wife and onto himself. Or the woman comes down with the flu, and her husband gets angry. He doesn't want his life disrupted, nor does he want to take care of her. He wants her to be focusing on him.

A friend was working in her office at home when her husband walked in and said, "I've been running all over the house trying to tell you goodbye." Notice how his focus was on himself, even though he was trying to be thoughtful of his wife.

"If you have knowledge, let others light their candles with it."

Winston Churchill

A Plan of Attack

Everyone needs to be center stage some of the time. However, always trying to grab attention by talking too much or interrupting or shifting the attention will not bring you success or happiness or make you closer to other people. If anything, it will drive others away.

If you know you talk too much, talk less. A good rule of thumb: Not more than two minutes of talking before you stop and let the other person make a comment, ask a question or change the topic of conversation. Remember also, silence is golden. Allow yourself and others some golden minutes.

Many women have said to me, "I know I talk too much."

If you are aware of the fact that you talk too much, talk less. Don't keep up this annoying behavior.

If you frequently interrupt, make a decision to be more conscious of not interrupting. Some years ago I interviewed hundreds of people about their marriages. I'd ask questions and they would talk. Over and over people told me how much they enjoyed the interview. I think it was because I was respectful of their stories and I listened with little interruption.

Life is sometimes very hard. Why make it harder on yourself by feeling sad or angry or disappointed at another's good fortune? Why continually compete with others to be center stage? Wouldn't it be nice to feel good when you hear of someone else's success? Wouldn't it be nice to sit back and relax, and not always have to grab the spotlight?

CHAPTER 11

How Controlling Are You?

When I asked Gretchen how things were going in her marriage, she said, "It's the same. Sam's still trying to run my life.

"When we go to the grocery store, I like to read the labels, check out the fat grams. He says, 'Hurry up. Let's get going. You don't need to read that stuff. You're thin enough.'

"I tell Sam my thinness has nothing to do with reading the labels. I'm reading them for other health reasons."

> ***"As I grow older, I pay less attention to what men say. I just watch what they do."***
>
> Andrew Carnegie

Gretchen also told me this story.

"Sam came in the house and said, 'Your lilies of the valley are blooming. Did you forget to pick them?'

"I told him no, I hadn't forgotten. I was just busy. I'd get to them.

"It wasn't more than a few hours later and he's in my sewing room telling me again that the lilies are blooming.

"I said, 'Yes. I know.' In my head I thought, 'Stop trying to tell me what to do!'

"The following morning when I came into the kitchen there was a note from Sam on the table. It read, 'Pick lilies of the valley. Sam.'"

Gretchen said she was so annoyed by the note that she decided she was *not* going to pick the flowers.

Neither of these people realizes they have a control issue. Gretchen could have given up the fight by picking the flowers, which she had originally intended to do. Or she could have told Sam to go ahead and pick them. On the other hand, Sam needed to stop badgering Gretchen. Another option he had was to ask Gretchen if she minded if he picked the flowers.

Gretchen controls by being passive. Sam is an active controller, directing and telling his wife what to do.

> ***"You will never rise to a level higher than what comes out of your mouth."***
> Anonymous

Pushing to Have Your Own Way

One of the most common ways a person tries to control another is by telling them what to do. Now, a parent gets to instruct a child because the parent is responsible for teaching the child and the child is supported by the parent. A boss gets to direct a worker because the worker gets a paycheck, and that's part of the agreement. Ministers, priests, rabbis, policemen, therapists, doctors, nurses, lawyers and editors also get to tell people what to do on occasion. But for the most part, unless someone asks your opinion, telling others what to do is not productive and should not be part of your behavior.

Ask yourself: ***If my mate is driving, what gives me the right to tell him where to park? If my friend has decided to take a different job, what gives me the right to tell her she's wrong? If my husband is pruning the bushes, what gives me the right to tell him how to do it?***

Before you go off instructing, directing and giving helpful hints, ask if you really have this right. Does this person really want your feedback?

Temper tantrums are another favorite means of trying to gain control over another. You're unhappy with something, and you turn on your anger to force the other person into submission.

Incessant talkers are controllers. As long as someone is talking, they have your time. Maybe not your attention, but your time.

Mumblers are also controllers. Have you ever noticed how everyone has to lean forward to hear a mumbler? And even when you ask the person to please speak up, he doesn't.

I have a friend who pouts. When we get together and someone disagrees with him, his first response is to get aggressive by raising his voice and telling the other person he's wrong. If the person doesn't back down, he then closes up like a clam and refuses to talk. Make no mistake, refusing to talk is a way to try to control another.

I saw a man in group therapy who never would answer a question. You'd ask him something, and he'd go into some long dissertation. The other group members would say, "Answer the question" five or six times before he actually answered. It wasn't that he was searching for an answer; it was that he liked to make you wait. While we waited, he was in control.

One woman I worked with in therapy drove her husband nuts because she wouldn't make a decision. She wouldn't decide where she wanted to go on vacation, what kind of a car to buy, what movie to see or what restaurant she wanted to go to. While she hemmed-and-hawed, he waited, and she had the control. And if he made a suggestion, she found fault with it.

Why People Think It's Their Right to Control

"Do not judge your friend until you stand in his place."

Apples of Gold

Why do people try to control others?

Sometimes it stems from being a perfectionist. The person thinks she knows best. Because she thinks she knows best, she tries to get others to do things her way.

Sometimes a controlling person has low self-esteem. She hides her insecurity by telling others what to do.

An individual may try to control others because she lacks control of her own life. She dislikes her job, her house is in disarray and her marriage is in shambles.

Pride is often a factor. The person is so arrogant that he presumes it's his right to instruct and tell others what's best for them.

A Test: How Controlling Are You?

Most people don't think they're controlling. They see others as controlling. Take the following test to see how controlling you are. Answer each question with a yes or no. Pencil in your answers so you can refer to them. The results may surprise you.

Yes No

☐ ☐ 1. Have you often been accused of not contributing to a conversation or giving only one- or two-word answers when asked a question?

☐ ☐ 2. Do you talk too much?

☐ ☐ 3. Do you frequently offer unsolicited advice, telling people what restaurant to go to, what to order, where to shop, what kind of a car to buy?

☐ ☐ 4. Do you have trouble apologizing, or are you the last to apologize after an argument?

☐ ☐ 5. Do you pout and refuse to talk when you get angry?

☐ ☐ 6. Do you tell people you'll do something by a certain date and then not get it done?

☐ ☐ 7. When you want something done, does it have to be done NOW?

☐ ☐ 8. Do you frequently run late, making others wait?

☐ ☐ 9. Do you make social plans for your mate or family without discussing the arrangements first?

☐ ☐ 10. Have you been confronted about not sharing or giving enough information at home or on the job?

☐ ☐ 11. Are you often accused of not listening or not hearing?

☐ ☐ 12. Do you often jump in and finish another's story?

☐ ☐ 13. Do you usually have the last word in an argument?

☐ ☐ 14. Do you consider yourself a critical person?

☐ ☐ 15. Do you shout and yell to get your point across?

☐ ☐ 16. Have you been accused of mumbling and talking too softly?

☐ ☐ 17. Do you ask a friend or mate what he or she wants to do and then try to get the person to do what you want?

☐ ☐ 18. Do you ask someone what they might like as a gift and then give them something different, something you think is best?

☐ ☐ 19. Do you insist on being the perfect host and waiting on everyone?

☐ ☐ 20. Do you withhold compliments, hugs, sex and "I love yous"?

Every yes answer indicates controlling behavior. More than three yes answers indicates you are trying to run too many shows.

If you answered yes to numbers 3, 7, 12, 13, 14, 15, and 17, you actively seek control and are upfront with your bid to run someone else's life by offering advice, expecting people to meet your schedule, finishing people's stories, having the last word and throwing your anger around.

If you answered yes to numbers 1, 2, 4, 5, 6, 8, 9, 10, 11, 16, 18, 19, and 20, you are more subtle in your bid for control. Your behavior, however, can be just as infuriating, provocative and annoying.

If you desire good relationships with your fellow workers, your mate, your children, your friends, watch for controlling behavior and work to eradicate it. Remember too: If you're in control of yourself, you won't try to control others.

CHAPTER 12

Is Your Thinking Positive or Negative? Past, Present or Future Focused?

When you wake up in the morning, what are your first thoughts? Do you think about yesterday's disappointments? Are you already on the job talking to a colleague? Or do you think how wonderful the bed feels and how nice your pillow is?

As you're brushing your teeth, are you thinking about last night's television show? Are you making out your list of what you want to accomplish that day? Or do you feel the bristles of the brush and see the toothpaste foam in your mouth?

How much time do you spend thinking of the past? The present? The future?

12

> ***"You just think lovely wonderful thoughts and they lift you up in the air."***
>
> Peter Pan

Caught in the Past

I read a story about a man, Jimmie G., that I will never forget. The story was in the book *The Man Who Mistook His Wife for a Hat* by Oliver Sacks.

Jimmie G., age 45, had a neurological problem. Because of his problem, he had no recent memory. His doctor would talk with him and walk out of the room. When the doctor returned a few minutes later, Jimmie had no memory of ever having seen the doctor.

As Sacks wrote in his notes, ***"... so that whatever was said or shown to him was apt to be forgotten in a few seconds' time."***[17] ***"... He is a man without a past (or future), stuck in a constantly changing, meaningless moment."***[18]

Memory is what helps make you who you are. You build on the past. You call on it continually in the present. You use it to plan for the future. You can call forth the previous day or hold a conversation with a friend based on your past interactions. You can see your children, your mate, your work environment in your mind's eye. You can recall a disappointment or a vacation you took long ago. You remember how it feels to bite into an apple on a beautiful autumn day.

> ***"God cannot be solemn, or he would not have blessed man with the incalculable gift of laughter."***
>
> Pierre Augustin de Beaumarchais

• • •

When I started working with Denise, she told me her most happy times were in high school. She was a cheerleader, had a date for every occasion and had many good friends. Although not particularly interested in academics, she made good grades.

Shortly after high school she married, had a son and moved out of state. That's when her husband started abusing her. After a year, Denise divorced and moved home. For the past eight years she has been supporting herself and her son.

She came to see me because her boyfriend had left her, and she was feeling depressed and lonely. She was having trouble getting up in the morning to help her son off to school. She had lost a considerable amount of weight. Her friends and family were worried.

As we talked, Denise would tell me again and again, "The best part of my life is over. If only I could be back in high school."

Is it possible that, you, like Denise, are hurting yourself more by dwelling too much in the past?

When I see someone who focuses too much on the past, I will often relate the following passage by David Reynolds. It's from Reynolds' book *Water Bears No Scars*.

"A rushing stream of water flows around the obstacles that stand in its way. It doesn't stop to dwell on the injuries sustained by a projecting rock or a submerged log. It keeps moving toward its goal, encountering each difficulty as it appears, responding actively, then moving along downstream. The stream has no imagination to create unchanging stories of its existence. It washes away its own wounds in its present purposefulness. The water bears no scars."[19]

Hurrying to the Future

On the opposite side of those who are caught in the past are those who think only of the future. It's always the next paycheck, the next deal, the next sexual experience, the next purchase, the next golf game. They're so caught up in what they think is going to happen that they miss out on the present.

The husband of a couple we used to socialize with was always thinking of the future. We'd go to dinner before a play. But before we ordered, the guy would announce the time we had to leave. On leaving the restaurant, we had to drive fast to the theater so we could get a good parking space. Before the curtain came down, this fellow wanted to be out the door so we could beat the traffic, so he could hurry home, so he could get to sleep, so he could jump out of bed in the morning and race to the gym.

Don't get me wrong. It's important to think about the future some of the time. If you want to change jobs, you have to prepare a resumé that is to be used in the future. If your daughter's getting married, you have to plan the wedding. If you're running a company, you need to think five, ten years ahead. At the same time, you can miss the present because your thinking is too much in the future.

Often one of my students will say, "I'm taking five courses this semester. I want to get them out of the way so I can get on with my life." What he forgets is that his life is going on now. If he can see his education as a process instead of something to be gotten over, he'll have more enjoyment along the way.

• • •

"I have known a great many troubles — most of them never happened."

Mark Twain

Worriers are future-oriented people. They think, "I wonder if the plane will be on time ... I wonder if they'll give us our loan ... I wonder if he'll call?"

Some friends of ours who live on a farm have a perfect answer for worriers. They learned it from an old farmer who lived down the road. They asked his advice about a calf. "Do you think he'll live?" they queried anxiously. After studying the calf, the farmer said, "Either it will or it won't."

Later in the year the woman was worrying about how dry everything was and wondered when it would rain, so she asked the farmer, "Do you think it's going to rain?" His reply, "Either it will or it won't."

If you're caught worrying about the future, you can make use of this sentence. Sometimes when a family member brings up a worry, one of us will say, "Either it will or it won't." Always the comment brings a smile of recognition and pulls the person away from his worries and into the present.

Learning to Live in the Present

"Most of us are worrying about the future so much that we can't enjoy the present."

Harold Sherman

You should focus most of your thoughts on what you are doing in the present, because the present is really all you have. The past is gone and the future is not yet.

For example, while you're planting daisies, don't think about what happened yesterday at work, or what you're going to wear to the party four weeks from now. Think about the plant you're putting in the soil. Notice how its roots cling to the black container as you try to remove it. Feel the trowel in your hand as you dig hard into the dirt. Feel the temperature of the dirt as you place your plant in the ground. Observe the way the plant stands as you tap the dirt around its base. Step back and look at it in your garden. Enjoy. This is what it means to live in the present, in the now.

In his book *Handbook to Higher Consciousness*, Ken Keyes suggests:

"It is best not to hang out discussing the past or to let your consciousness dwell on the past, for the constant churning of your mind (and the torrent of words that issues from it) keeps you from fully experiencing the now moment in your life.

"Nor will you generate the best future for yourself by being constantly preoccupied with thoughts of the future ...

"The real solutions to the problems in your life will come to you when you ... become fully tuned in to the people and things that are around you."[20]

Living in the present means you allow yourself to ***"experience everything in an accepting, relaxed and conscious way."***[21]

Is Your Thinking Positive or Negative?

When presented with a situation, some people immediately think negative thoughts while others see the silver lining and think positive thoughts. In the next few stories you will meet both positive and negative thinkers. As you read, ask yourself: ***Am I like this person? Do I view life from a positive or negative frame of reference?***

Recently I received a telephone call at my office from a father who was very upset. He told me that his son and his son's family would not be joining him and his wife on Christmas day.

The father had invited another family, who was not related, to spend Christmas with them. When the son found out that another family would be at his parents' home, his thoughts were negative. Christmas wasn't going to be as much fun. He'd have to be on guard. Conversations would be superficial. He wouldn't be able to relax. Based on his negative assessment of what was going to happen, he felt angry and jealous. He

"Do you see difficulties in every opportunity or opportunities in every difficulty?"

Apples of Gold

then translated his thinking and feeling into behavior. He called his dad and cancelled.

What's interesting is that the son could just as easily have thought positively about the situation. He might have said, "The more, the merrier." He could have looked for a common denominator with the other family. What did the man and woman do for a living? Did they have children? His children would probably love to have playmates. He might have put himself in the other family's shoes: How nice it was for them to be invited for Christmas dinner.

• • •

Every once in a while when my friend Carol is in the vicinity of my office, she'll stop for a visit. If I'm free, we'll have a cup of coffee. The other day she came by. When she first drove up to the building, she said to herself, "Oh, my. Now they have underground parking. And they have new landscaping. How nice." Once she was inside the building, she thought, "Why they've even changed the walls and the wallpaper."

She then realized she was in the wrong building.

It's revealing, however, that when she was trying to make sense of the building, her thinking was positive. She ooh'd and ah'd about all the nice changes. When she finally got to my office, she was laughing hysterically.

A person who operates from a negative frame of reference might have handled the situation quite differently. When she saw the underground parking, she might have thought, "What are they doing making underground parking? This building was fine as it was." When she walked inside the building she might have said, "I can't believe they changed the walls and the wallpaper. What a waste of money." And when she realized her mistake, she might have thought, "Boy, am I a dummy."

> ***"The world is moving so fast these days that the man who says it can't be done is generally interrupted by someone doing it."***
>
> Harry Emerson Fosdick

• • •

I asked a secretary to take an incident that had happened at work recently, and come up with both a positive and a negative way of looking at it. The situation she chose — receiving a memo that a seminar was going to be held the following week and everyone was expected to attend.

Her negative thoughts: "I don't want to go. I've got too much to do. I can't give up a day. I've already taken a seminar on this subject."

Her positive thoughts: "Maybe a day thinking about something else will energize me. In truth, I always learn something. Maybe I'll get some tips on handling people who don't get to work on time."

Take a moment now and think about an incident that's happened to you recently.

Come up with three negative thoughts about the incident.

____

____

____

Now come up with three positive thoughts.

____

____

____

This exercise illustrates the way you can cause yourself to feel content or annoyed, based on the thoughts you choose to think.

There's Always Another Interpretation

Most people operate under the assumption that the way they see life is the way it is. This assumption, however, is not true. Each person sees things from his own reference point, which is almost always different from another's frame of reference.

For example, a 29-year-old woman smokes. She has been smoking for years but has never let her parents know. In fact, she's gone to great lengths to hide her smoking. She says,

"I don't tell my parents because it would cause them to feel anxious about my health." A friend of hers thinks differently. He says, "She doesn't tell her parents because she's afraid they'll lecture and try to extract a no-smoking promise."

Neither of these people is right or wrong. They simply interpret the situation differently.

• • •

"Our organization has recently been reorganized," said Beth. "As a consequence, mail gets delivered to us that doesn't belong in our department. When I find a piece that isn't ours, I look up the person's name in our directory, find out what department it should go to, and send it on its way.

"The other people in our department think I'm silly for doing this. When they go through the mail and find a piece that doesn't belong to us, they send it back to the mailroom. They think it's the mailroom's job."

Who's right? It depends on your thinking.

• • •

"An optimist may see a light where there is none, but why must the pessimist always run to blow it out?"

Michel
De Saint-Pierre

A partner in a company told me that when a customer calls and says, "Your equipment is not working," he immediately thinks, "I wonder what we did wrong? I wonder if the design is faulty?" On the other hand, when his partner hears there's a problem, the partner says, "The customer must be doing something wrong."

This same man said he and his partner were at a bank borrowing money recently, and one of the bankers asked some personal questions. "My partner immediately said, 'You don't need to know that.' I, on the other hand, would have given the banker all the information he asked for and probably would have asked what more he needed."

• • •

When my business partner Serra told people she joined the Peace Corps and was leaving for Romania, she got mixed reviews. Some said, "How wonderful. What an adventure you'll have." Others said, "I can't believe anybody would want to do such a thing."

Misinterpreting Reality

Sometimes instead of simply perceiving things differently, you actually misinterpret reality, as the young woman did in the next story.

My dad had just had surgery and was in the intensive care unit. My mother and I were sitting in the hospital lobby waiting until we could see him. The two of us were talking and laughing and enjoying ourselves, I think for the first time in days, because we felt Dad was going to be OK.

Across the lobby was a young woman with two small children. As Mom and I talked, I noticed that the youngest child was giving his mother a hard time — fussing and tugging to get away from her grip. The mother was holding onto the child's sleeve with one hand and trying to balance a plate of cookies in her other hand.

I must have looked in another direction for a few seconds when all of a sudden the young woman was standing in front of us. She leaned forward and demanded in a loud, mean voice, "Are you having a good time?"

I was baffled. I turned my head around thinking the woman must be chastising someone behind me. But no one was there. The woman then stormed past with her children and disappeared down the hall.

Mom and I concluded that the woman must have decided that we were enjoying her predicament. She saw us laughing and looking in her direction and assumed that we were talking about her. She had misinterpreted reality.

• • •

One day I was in the car alone, sitting at a stop sign. All of a sudden I felt a tremendous jolt and my head was thrust forward. Immediately I thought, "I've been shot." I also thought, "Why would they want to shoot me?" I was confused, bewildered.

As I started to get out of the car, a woman rushed up to me and said, "Are you okay? I'm so sorry." I realized then that I hadn't been shot, but I'd been rear-ended. I'd misinterpreted reality.

To this day I'm not sure why I jumped to the conclusion

CASE STUDY

12

"You grow up the day you have your first real laugh — at yourself."

Apples of Gold

that I was shot when a more plausible explanation was that someone had run into the back of my car. Too many movies? Too many violent stories in the newspaper?

• • •

A man and wife went to a wedding. During the ceremony he commented to his wife, "My, this is a fancy wedding." After the wedding they went to the country club for the reception. When they arrived, he noticed that the bridesmaids were now in different colored dresses. He thought, "This *really is* a fancy wedding. They even changed their dresses." Once in the receiving line facing the bride and groom, the couple realized they were at the wrong reception. The man had misread the situation, but notice how he tried to make reality fit his thinking.

More Out-of-Balance Thinking

There are three additional ways your thinking may cause you and others needless pain. First, there is overgeneralizing. If you've ever taken an incident and put too much importance on it or blown it out of proportion, you were overgeneralizing.

For example, Judy thinks that when she finds a man and gets married, everything in her life is going to be perfect. Of course, it won't. What Judy is doing is taking one event, marriage, and making it the be-all and end-all for her happiness.

• • •

"A man is what he thinks about all day long."

Ralph Waldo Emerson

I know an architect who missed out on a job. It turned out he was the company's second choice. The last time I talked to him, he was miserable. He kept saying, "I'll never get a job in my field."

It's bad enough to be rejected, but he thinks that this is the end of his career. What he's doing is overgeneralizing.

It's normal to have some bad feelings when things don't work out as planned, but overgeneralizing gives too much weight to an incident.

As Reynolds writes, ***"We can build in unnecessary pain in our lives by creating tragedies when there are only events."***[22]

Have you built in unnecessary pain in your life? When?

> ***"An open mind leaves a chance for someone to drop a worthwhile thought in it."***
>
> Apples of Gold

Jumping to Conclusions

Another way you may cause yourself bad feelings is by jumping to a negative conclusion. For example:

Your husband turns on the radio when the two of you get into the car, and you jump to the conclusion that he doesn't like talking to you.

You see your supervisor talking and laughing with a co-worker and you think she must like your co-worker better than you.

You have a fun time with a new date, and because he doesn't call you the following day, you're sure he didn't enjoy himself.

Your boss says she wants to talk with you, and you think she's going to call you on the carpet for something.

Are you guilty of jumping to conclusions?

Obsessing

You can also create needless suffering by obsessing — replaying an incident in your mind over and over. For example, Walter confronted his supervisor at a meeting several weeks ago. Now all he can think about is the argument that ensued. He rehashes what he said and what the supervisor said. He thinks of things he might have said. And sometimes he thinks, "Why on earth didn't I keep my mouth shut?"

• • •

A friend shared with me that she obsesses on her mother, who died when she was six years old.

"It will be around Mother's Day and I'll go to the store to buy my mother-in-law a card. As I'm reading the cards, I think about what card I would have sent to my mother. Then I think, 'I don't have a mother.' After I leave the store, I go over and over this thought and feel awful.

"If something happens with my children, good or bad, I flip to the loss-of-my-mother channel. I think, 'I don't have a mother to share this event with.'

"After I run all this out in my head, I'm miserable. When I've had enough misery, I get busy. I clean a drawer. I call a friend and listen to her problems. I get into my life. I stop obsessing."

> ***"Things turn out best for the people who make the best of the way things turn out."***
>
> John Wooden

• • •

Every day you're bombarded with thousands of thoughts. For example: I need to have the car inspected ... I wonder how Mom's doing? ... I hate my legs ... What if I don't make quota? ... Why can't my children be nicer to me? ... If only he'd stop smoking, he's killing himself ... If only my boss wouldn't always be looking over my shoulder ... I've got to start exercising ... I need to get gas.

In the book *How Can I Help?* the authors tell us,

"Our thoughts are always happening ... And they are all constantly calling for our attention: 'Think of me.' 'Notice me.' 'Attend to me.'

"As each thought passes, either we attend to it or we don't. While we can't stop the thoughts themselves, we can stop our awareness from being snared by each one."[23]

Are you causing yourself needless pain by obsessing on certain thoughts?

Which Is More Important — Thoughts, Feelings or Behavior?

Which is more important — your thoughts, feelings or behavior? All three are uniquely important. All three determine who you are.

Sometimes you think a thought or someone says something to you, and you attach no particular feeling to the thought. Other times you have an almost instantaneous response to a thought and feelings explode within you in less than a second. If your interpretation of the situation is positive, you'll experience a sense of well-being and feel pleased, perhaps even joyful. If your interpretation of the event is negative, you're likely to feel frustrated, annoyed, angry. Or you may feel sad, defeated and helpless. You may or may not choose to act on your thoughts and feelings.

"Thought is a sculptor who can create the person you want to be."

Henry David Thoreau

Suppose you have the thought, "I haven't heard from Sandra in a while. Your next thoughts, "I wonder if she's irritated with me? Did I do something to offend her? I've called her the last three times. Maybe she only calls when she wants my help. She doesn't really care about me and my life. Well, I don't need her as a friend. I have plenty of other people who want to be my friend."

As you're thinking these thoughts that took less than a few seconds, feelings are also being created. In this case you're probably going to feel hurt and angry.

Now, you may choose to act on your thoughts and feelings by deciding never to call Sandra. You may act on your thoughts and feelings by calling her and picking a fight. Or you could decide that you'll stop this line of thinking, focus on something else, and your feelings will dissipate.

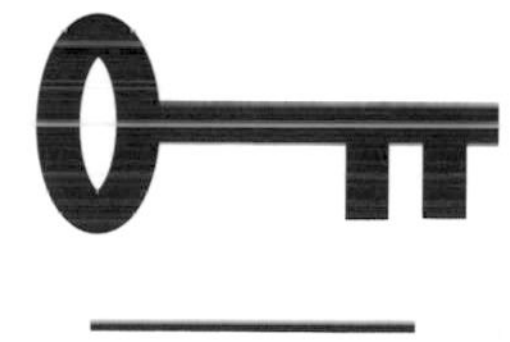

I believe you can hurt yourself and others most by your behavior. But you can also cause yourself great harm by thinking negative thoughts, which will most assuredly translate into negative feelings.

I am not a therapist who thinks feelings are the most important part of you. I don't hold feelings up for admiration. I don't ask clients how they feel when they report losing a job or having a fight with their mate. I can see how they feel. I hear their feelings in their voice, see their feelings in their eyes, their face, their body posture. I know when they are sad, annoyed, frustrated, pleased, happy.

Feelings are integral to our humanness. Feeling sad shows that you are vulnerable. Feeling fear exposes your insecurities. Feeling anger indicates your desire to control and sometimes your strength. Feeling guilt helps you police your actions. Feeling lonely shows your hunger for attachment to another human being. Feeling happiness and joy indicate your capacity for pleasure, love, and intimacy.

It is your thinking, however, that makes you most human. It is your thinking that generates most of your feelings. It is your thinking that directs your actions and keeps your behavior in check. It is your thinking that generates the feelings that allow you to tend to your wants and needs and to transcend your own wants and needs for those of others.

CHAPTER 13

Are You Aware of Your Psychological Addictions and How They Run Your Life?

> ***"The secret of your future is hidden in your daily routine."***
>
> Mike Murdock

Our son Paul was graduating from high school. We were giving him a party. Everyone in the family had worked hard to get the house shipshape. About 10 minutes before the guests were to arrive, I did a quick check of the rooms. When I went into one of the bathrooms, I noticed the glass shower door had a film on it. I immediately grabbed a cloth, took off my high heels, climbed stocking feet into the bathtub and went to work on the film.

As I was cleaning, a very rational thought popped into my head: "Doris, what are you doing? Everything looks great. Stop."

I was addicted to perfection. Everything had to be perfect, including the shower door.

The problem with thinking that everything must be perfect is that it's out of whack. It carries too much importance, while other things, including people, take on a secondary importance. What I could have done with those 10 minutes was congratulate our son and talk with him about all his accomplishments in the past four years. I could have talked with him about how it felt to be graduating and getting ready to go off to college. I could have enjoyed a glass of wine with my husband or simply sat with my feet up and savored the moment.

Often when people hear the word "addiction," they think, "That's not me — I don't use drugs, I'm not an addict," or "I don't have a problem with alcohol," or "I'm not a binge eater." You may not have these problems, but what I have found is that most people are addicted to someone or something in their life.

What exactly does it mean to have a psychological addiction? It means you have a craving, a fixation, an obsession for someone or something in your life. You tell yourself that in order to be happy you must have this particular thing. It can be a certain salary, a promotion, a relationship, a contract, a perfectly kept house, a piece of jewelry, a certain weight, a certain food. When the craving is not satisfied, you experience great discomfort. You may feel anxious, sad, depressed, angry or a combination of these emotions.

Uncovering Your Addictions

To uncover some of your addictions, answer the following questions with a yes or no. You may want to pencil in your answers, since I'll refer to them later.

Yes	No	
☐	☐	1. Do you avoid going out with people in order to be able to stay on your diet?
☐	☐	2. Are you unable to have a good time with friends if someone in the group is more attractive, better dressed, more educated or better off financially?
☐	☐	3. Do you have trouble making decisions?
☐	☐	4. Are you especially attracted to people who have money?
☐	☐	5. Do you insist on being the one who chooses most of the gifts in your family?
☐	☐	6. Do you drink more than six cups of coffee, tea or soda each day? Do you immediately pour yourself a drink when you walk in the house at night? Do you find yourself feeling annoyed if you are at a party or in a restaurant that does not serve alcohol?
☐	☐	7. Do you frequently have to have something new — a shirt, a tie, shoes, makeup — to feel good about yourself?

☐ ☐ 8. Do you find yourself becoming hostile in your tone of voice when someone says something you don't agree with? Do you allow yourself to lose your temper several times a week?

☐ ☐ 9. Do you usually have to have the last word in an argument?

☐ ☐ 10. Are you in a job that you know you should leave? Or are you in a relationship that you know you should end?

☐ ☐ 11. If a friend stops by unexpectedly, are you more focused on how you look or how your house looks than on talking to your friend?

☐ ☐ 12. Do you often think that your mate's, children's or friends' lives could be better if they would just do such and such?

☐ ☐ 13. Do you measure your success by how much money you make?

☐ ☐ 14. Do you weigh too much or drink too much?

☐ ☐ 15. Once you see something in a store or a catalogue, do you spend a good deal of time thinking about the item and plotting how you will get it?

Every yes answer indicates a possible addiction.

Now let's see in what areas you're most likely to be addicted.

Numbers 1, 2, 7, and 11 indicate you're placing too much importance on appearance. Number 2 also indicates you operate from a competitive frame of reference, frequently assessing your worth against that of others.

Numbers 3 and 10 signify a security addiction

Numbers 4 and 13 suggest a money addiction.

Numbers 5, 8, 9, and 12 indicate a desire to control the lives of others. A "yes" to number 8 also indicates you have an anger problem.

Numbers 6 and 14 suggest a food or drink addiction.

Number 15 suggests you are addicted to spending money and acquiring things.

"You will never change your life until you change something you do daily."

Mike Murdock

13

CASE STUDY

Now I'd like to introduce you to a number of people, each of whom has an addictive behavioral pattern. As you read their stories, ask yourself — ***Am I like any of these people? Do I have the same addictive pattern?***

Lucy works in a miserable environment. Every time I see her, she tells me she hates her job. It's boring. She also dislikes her boss. "The man won't make a decision," she says. "And when he does, it's because someone has browbeat him into it."

Because Lucy's been with the company for so many years, she's afraid to move on. She's concerned about losing benefits. And what happens if she doesn't like her next job? Or what if she takes another job and gets fired? Her addiction to security keeps her stuck in a job she dislikes, working with someone she does not respect. Her need to feel secure costs her countless hours, days and months of worry and frustration.

Marc is in his second marriage. His first wife ran off with his best friend, a hurt he has never gotten over or resolved. Marc's now remarried and driving his second wife nuts. He's always checking on her — calling to see where she's been, where she's going. Their last blow-up was triggered when his wife went with a group of friends to a concert and got home later than expected.

Marc has a security addiction. His addiction causes him a great deal of worry, fear and sadness. His addiction is also destroying his marriage.

Jill knew walking down the aisle that she wasn't in love with her soon-to-be husband. But she was tired of scraping by. "Even if he's boring," she said, "I'll make the best of it." Jill has compromised herself for her addiction — financial security.

I've been seeing Patty on and off in therapy for two years. Every time I see her, she asks me why her boyfriend left her when they were such a perfect couple. She wants to go over each date and all the fun things they did together. She tells me she's never met a man as nice as her former boyfriend. She wakes up thinking about him and goes to bed thinking about him. She believes she can't be happy without him.

Because he's out of the picture, she feels unhappy, sad, depressed. What she can't see is that she's wasted two years of her life thinking about someone who's not coming back. Patty is addicted to the past and feeling miserable.

I watched a man arguing with his wife over how much money she pays the boy who cleans the stalls in their barn. She thinks the boy is worth $4.50 an hour. He thinks the boy should be paid only $4. He also demands to know why his wife thinks it's her place to feed the boy lunch when he can bring his own. Her exasperated retort: "I only give him a sandwich and a soda."

The man's addiction — money. Paying bills makes him nervous and anxious. He constantly argues with his wife about her spending. His money addiction is making him and those around him very unhappy.

Some people have a money addiction of another sort. They frequently talk about how much something costs, how expensive everything is, how they're not sure they'll make ends meet. If they are given a present, they calculate its worth. If they learn that a friend has bought a new car, they wonder how he could afford it. Their focus — money.

Sandra is extremely conscious of her looks. She spends most of her time and money on clothes, jewelry and makeup. If she sees a woman she thinks is prettier, she feels bad about herself. Sandra frets about her veins, her wrinkles, her weight, her hair, the fact that she's getting older. She is obsessed with her appearance.

Some people are addicted to shopping. They can't go a week without running to the mall to make a purchase. It's a shirt, a book, a belt, a pair of blue jeans, a piece of sporting equipment, a kitchen utensil, lipstick, cologne, earrings, a tie. Shopping makes them feel good. They use shopping as a pick-me-up when they're down. They shop to celebrate. It doesn't matter that they can't pay off their charges.

Other people are addicted to having things. They make a purchase, and then they immediately start thinking about what they can buy next. They are never satisfied. They are insatiable. They can't seem to get filled up. They have four televisions, three stereos, three VCRs, a basement full of

"If at first you don't succeed, you're running about average."

M.H. Alderson

exercise equipment that they never use and more camera equipment than a professional.

Another addiction you may have — everything should go as planned. If someone tells you she's going to bring you a book, you expect her to do it. If a repair person tells you he'll be there at 1:00, you expect him to arrive at 1:00. If you go on vacation, you expect no hitches. When expectations are not met, you become annoyed and angry. I call this "The Way It Should Be Addiction."

"Quitting smoking is the easiest thing in the world. I've done it hundreds of times."

Mark Twain

People with this addiction also are obsessed with controlling and changing the lives of others. If another person has a problem, they immediately try to solve it. They watch their children's and their friends' lives, and they think, "If he or she would just behave differently." They come up with little programs and schemes to help others improve. Unhappiness comes when others do not follow their advice.

Shirley has become addicted to gambling. She works as a bartender. When the bar closes, the employees sit around and play poker. "It's a way to unwind," she says. She may lose $100, all the money she made that evening. On her days off, she goes riverboat gambling. She cannot afford the money she's losing or the time she is giving to her new addiction.

Some people are psychologically addicted to alcohol. They think life is no fun without it. When they walk in the house, the first thing they do is open a can of beer or pour themselves a scotch. They wouldn't think of making dinner without having several glasses of wine as they cook. If alcohol isn't served at a social function, they're disappointed. They avoid restaurants that don't serve liquor. They choose their friends on the basis of their drinking habits. They may or may not be physically addicted.

I know a woman who drank two 64-ounce bottles of cola every day. That's 16 glasses of soda a day. Another woman I saw in therapy drank 30 cups of tea a day! Some people smoke two to three packs of cigarettes a day.

Set out 16 glasses of soda and 60 cigarettes on a table to see what this actually looks like.

Are you addicted to coffee? Tea? Cola? Cigarettes?

How Are Your Addictions Interfering With Your Life?

Once you recognize your addictions, ask yourself the following:

1. How does this desire drive my life?

   ____

   ____

2. How does this addiction hurt me?

   ____

   ____

3. How does it hurt my relationships with others?

   ____

   ____

It's important to have goals and dreams. There's nothing wrong with wanting an orderly house, money in the bank, a new outfit, a good dinner, a graduate degree, a better job, a relationship. But it's equally important that your desires do not continually dominate your thinking. If you allow them to, you'll miss out on the moment, you'll miss out on your life.

How Do You Quell Your Addictions?

Ken Keyes, in his book *Handbook to Higher Consciousness*, suggests working on your addictions by viewing them as preferences. You reprogram your thinking so you are not restless or unhappy if a desire is not realized. You change your desires to preferences.

For example, let's say you're addicted to making a certain income. If you continually say, "I have to make this amount,"

"Wealth consists not in having great possessions but in having few wants."

Epicurus

or "I'm going to make this amount," and you fail to accomplish your goal, you will experience sadness and perhaps anger. You may get into blaming your wife because you took time off for a vacation. You may wind up feeling jealous because your partner made more money.

But if you say instead, "I *prefer* to make this amount," and you fail to make it, you won't set yourself up for bad feelings.

When people have a preference instead of a desire, they don't get all hot and bothered when it doesn't come to fruition.

The other day I was waiting for the electrician. He was supposed to arrive at noon, but it was almost 4:00, and he hadn't come. I started thinking, "I hope he remembers. I want that light fixed. I bet he forgot. Maybe he won't come at all because it's such a little job." Ay-yay-yay.

When I got hold of myself, I said, "My *preference* is that the electrician come today so the light gets fixed." As soon as I used the word "preference," I freed myself. I wasn't emotionally invested.

• • •

I recently had an antique cupboard shipped to our home. In the shipping it was damaged. Knowing how upset I can get when things don't go the way I think they should, I had already talked to myself about the possibility that the piece could be damaged. When I saw that one of the panes of old glass was broken and the door was sprung, I said in my head, "My preference is that the cabinet would not have been damaged." Once I said this, I left the past and was able to move to the present and check out the yellow pages for a cabinetmaker. Even my daughter said, "Mom, you're so calm. Aren't you mad about your cabinet?" I said, "No, I just have to find someone to fix it."

Try it. It's amazing how it works. Take something you're worrying and agonizing over, and turn it into a preference. I prefer to get the living room painted by next Saturday. I prefer to be married. I prefer my company win the contract. I prefer to make quota. I prefer that the house stay clean.

Eastern philosophy teaches that unhappiness comes from desires. If you quell your desires, instead of always trying to satisfy them, you'll feel more peaceful. I guarantee.

CHAPTER 14

Do You Talk to God?

Do you pray? Do you talk to God?

My earliest recollection of talking to God is of kneeling with my mother and sister before bedtime at the side of our bed. We'd start with the "Our Father," and then we'd pray for special intentions. One of us would say, "God, take care of Grandma," or "God, please help all the people who are hungry."

As I grew, I continued talking to God. I'd ask God to please, please have Sally invite me to her birthday party, or please let me be elected to student government. During grade school I realized that if Betsy asked God to help her be elected and I asked God to be elected to the same position, there was a problem. So I'd add, "If Thy will be done." I was hoping, of course, that my will would be done.

Besides going to church on Sunday and special days during the year, our family also prayed together once a month. My dad would say, "We're going to pray today." My sister and I would roll our eyes at each other. Reluctantly we'd go into my parents' bedroom, where all four of us would kneel around the bed and Dad would lead the prayers. Despite my initial resistance to getting on the hard floor and praying, I must admit I always felt good afterward. Secretly I thought it was pretty neat that our family all knelt down together and prayed.

As I got older, I continued to keep up my relationship with God. I'd ask God to get me dates and help with tests. At that time I still had a take-care-of-me view of God. He was my Father in heaven, and He was supposed to take care of me like a good father does. At the same time, I had biblical backing.

> ***"God gives every bird its food, but he does not throw it into the nest."***
>
> J.G. Holland

"And all things, whatever ye shall ask in prayer, believing, ye shall receive."[24]

Matthew 21:22

I also made regular bargains with God, such as, "If you help me pass algebra, I'll say a hundred prayers for the sick."

> ***"Prayer is our invisible means of support."***
>
> Anonymous

I think the first time I became angry with God was when I missed out on a modeling job. Silly, huh? That wasn't the last time, however. I'd get righteous about something I'd hear on the news, and I'd tell God to get busy and do something.

After our second child was born, I had complications and was near death. I was being wheeled to surgery, and I remember thinking, "Well, God, if I don't wake up, I'll see you in heaven. Please take care of my family." Maybe I was naive, but, because I felt a connection with God, because talking to God has always been an integral part of my life, I was not afraid of death.

Today I still use formalized prayer, usually before I go to sleep. But during the day I just talk to God. I ask Him to help people who have difficult lives. I ask Him to help people who have problems with their anger. If I'm annoyed at someone, I'll pray for the person. This helps me let go of my irritation.

I also say, "Thank you, God," many times each day. I give thanks for my gentle, loving husband and wonderful children. I thank God all the time for giving us our two boys and then a girl years later. I thank God for letting my parents live for so many years. I thank God for a soft rain, a sunny day, a beautiful sunset. Lately, I've been thanking God for helping me write this book.

In therapy, I never shared the fact that I prayed. I'd give people all sorts of assignments but never prayer. Then I started seeing people who were trying to cope with the death of a child. They were in unbearable pain.

They'd ask me if the pain would ever go away. I'd shake my head no, but tell them it would lessen in time. I'd listen to their stories. Sometimes I'd wrap a blanket around them and just hold them tightly as they cried. Sometimes I'd have a couple hold each other. I recall one woman who came every week to cry. She'd curl up like a baby and weep. I felt helpless seeing her pain. Then one day I suggested that perhaps if she would pray, talk to God, she would get some relief. And she did. I now routinely suggest prayer as a way to get through problems and regain hope.

The Benefits of Prayer

I believe prayer has numerous benefits. If you have faith and believe in God, why not have a conversation with Him? Certainly you carry on conversations regularly in your head with various people. Why not God? He's the most accepting and forgiving friend you could possibly have.

Prayer helps you feel safe. It's like when you were little and you ran to Mom because you were afraid, and she said, "It'll be all right." That's what prayer does.

I think people who pray are more loving, compassionate and forgiving. It's hard to hate when you've been talking to God.

When people pray, they often report feeling less anxious and more peaceful. The fact that the electricity goes off or a friend makes a hurtful remark seems less important.

Prayer has a calming effect. It gives you strength and courage to face an existing problem or a tough decision. Praying helps you close off past regrets and future wants. It quells your obsessional thoughts. Prayer is steadying and adds balance to your life. It empowers you to feel more in control of yourself. It gives you the courage to let go of those things you can't control. Prayer calls on you to be responsible to yourself and to others. Praying is good therapy.

Sometimes when I look at the mountains or think of my family, I swell with feelings of strength, warmth and love. I take a deep breath and it's as though everything is right with the world. At that moment I want to share that feeling of intimacy. Who better to share it with than my friend God? "What a great day, God. Thanks."

"To see God in everything makes life the greatest adventure there is."

Apples of Gold

Who Prays?

"Prayer changes things. Prayer changes you!"
Anonymous

There have been a number of recent surveys which validate that Americans are becoming a more prayerful people and that people find praying helpful in their daily lives. In 1992, *Newsweek* reported that 91 percent of women pray while 85 percent of men pray.[25]

A Gallup survey for *Life*[26] in 1994 reported the following:

- 87 percent of people said they prayed once a week.
- 95 percent of people said their prayers are answered. It's not that they specifically got what they had prayed for, but they felt more hopeful and peaceful.
- 98 percent of the people who pray said they prayed for their families, and 92 percent prayed for forgiveness.
- 86 percent said praying made them better people.

Some Comments from Those Who Pray

I talked to a number of people from various religions about prayer. Here is what they had to say.

"When I pray, it makes me more accountable to myself. I feel more protected from making mistakes, from choosing things that are not good for me. I feel on the right path. I know God listens when I pray. The prayer I say the most is 'Help me be who you would have me be.'"

A wife, mother, and student

"I pray because I can't make it without God. I think there are a lot of things in life that I can't control. I pray for strength, courage, wisdom, the gift of letting go and not trying to control people I love. A lot of times I feel anxious that a family member won't make the right decision, so I pray a lot about that. I turn that over to God. I ask that He takes care of them and gives me the grace to let it go. I pray for my boyfriend, who has a troubled relationship with his son. I pray for good health, and I pray that if my health fails, I'll have the strength to handle it. I pray for the gift to enjoy life.

"I go to church every Sunday and once during the week. I take a few moments in the day and put myself with God. I no longer use a lot of formalized prayer. I just talk to God. When I see flowers or a blue sky, I say, 'This is God's goodness.'"

A psychotherapist

"Prayer for me is usually making a request of God for other people or for me. If someone is sick, I ask that they get better. I pray for people to be safe on a trip. I pray that things work and will go well in my business. I usually pray in the morning or at night. I feel less anxious when I pray."

A company president

"I pray in my head, I pray at church, I pray in the car. I talk to God in the middle of the night about my family, my health. I belong to a prayer group. We meet once a week to say prayers and study the Bible. When I pray, I ask for patience, a good day at work. I thank God for all I have. I'm a very impatient, anxious person, and when I pray, I become calm. I have a horrible fear of flying and sometimes I have to fly. The last time I flew, I was in the air praying like mad. My prayer group was on the ground praying for me. It was the easiest flight I've ever had."

An insurance adjuster

• • •

"A story is told of a child who goes out to the woods each day. His mother asks where he is going, and he tells her he is going to be with God. Day after day this goes on until finally she says, 'You know, son. God is the same everywhere.'

He responds, 'I know. But I'm not.'

"Prayer is where we go to feel our connection to God."[27]

"The greatest pleasure I know is to do a good action by stealth, and to have it found out by accident."

Charles Lamb

How to Start Using Prayer

There are many ways to pray to God. For some, prayer is simply sitting quietly and listening for God. Others find formal prayer more helpful. Some start with formal prayer and then listen. Some people read the Bible, or the Siddur, or other inspirational material. Many people talk to God as they would any other friend.

Sometimes people think they're too busy to stop and pray. I always say you can pray anywhere. You can pray sitting at a stop sign, brushing your teeth, exercising on the floor. I read of a woman who would walk through her neighborhood and pray for the occupants of each house as she passed.

If you'd like to start praying, ask a friend for his or her favorite prayer. Some well-loved prayers are the "Lord's Prayer"; the "Hail Mary"; the "Shema" which begins, ***"Hear O Israel, the Lord our God, the Lord is One...";***[28] the "Serenity Prayer"; and "Psalm 23," which begins, ***"The Lord is my shepherd; I shall not want... ."***[29]

Start saying a prayer each morning, or during the day, or at night. Start reading the Bible or a prayer book. Try talking to God in your head as you would anyone else — "Hi God, it's me." Or sit quietly, and listen for God.

No one has to live without the help of prayer.

CHAPTER 15

Living in a State of Maturity, Contentment and Happiness

"Believe that life is worth living and your belief will help create the fact."

William James

15

Remember the time you got your driver's license? Did you think you were all grown up?

How about when you moved away from home, got your own apartment, got married? Did you think you were grown up then?

What about after you had your first child? That's a wake-up call. Did this make you a grown-up person?

You lose a grandparent. One of your parents dies, your mate leaves, you lose a friend, a job. Is this what being grown up is all about?

You have children in high school. One of them comes home drunk. You don't like your daughter's boyfriend. Your kids won't get off the telephone, and you can't sleep. Every time your teenager has the car, you pray, "God, please don't let anything happen." You're starting to turn gray. Is this what it means to be mature?

Your children are out of the nest. You helped a good friend bury her brother. You're starting to notice: the world is changing. More and more people are younger. You look in the mirror and think, "I wonder how old people think I am?" You decide to start exercising again. You decide to go back to playing the piano. You're becoming more patient when you have to wait at the post office. You don't dwell on an insult. You're starting to mature.

Somewhere along the way you've come to the realization that life is hard. People suffer. Not everyone thinks like you do. Fighting and bickering are ridiculous — there are better ways to get your point across. It's not important to have a new dress for the dance. And so what if the cat throws up on your new carpet. You'll get a rag and clean it up. You are coming of age.

Does anyone reach full maturity? I think probably not. I believe it's something you have to work toward your entire life.

A Maturity Checklist

For the last few years I've been taking notes on how someone who has reached full maturity would live his or her life. I've thought about how the person would think and feel and behave. I've come up with a list of behaviors that bespeak maturity. If you can put a checkmark by 95 percent of the items, you're almost there.

So get your pencil and start checking!

☐ 1. You understand that life is hard, but you also realize that you have had some satisfactions and joy along the way.

☐ 2. You know that life is not fair, and sometimes bad things happen to good people.

☐ 3. You do not make more than three critical comments per week.

☐ 4. You do not lose your temper: no screaming, name-calling, pouting. You have learned to manage your anger.

☐ 5. You do not obsess about an old hurt or disappointment. You have come to understand that you can forgive almost anything.

☐ 6. You do what you say you will do. Amen. Period.

☐ 7. You always take others into account before making a decision.

☐ 8. You take yourself into account before making a decision.

☐ 9. You allow yourself to feel intimate many times each day — you laugh, notice the sunset, breathe in deeply and enjoy the sensation.

☐ 10. You can admit to three incidents in your life that you mishandled, causing yourself and others pain. (Review those incidents now.)

☐ 11. You apologize when you've made a mistake and work hard not to repeat it.

☐ 12. You do not have affairs, or one-night stands, or have sex with anyone you are not committed to.

☐ 13. You know how to listen. You are attentive and responsive. You ask questions when appropriate, and you do not shift the conversation to what you want to talk about.

☐ 14. You use a variety of options for dealing with emotional pain. You pray, call a friend, get busy on a project, do something for someone else, seek the help of a professional.

☐ 15. You behave in a nonjealous way despite the fact that sometimes you think jealous thoughts and have jealous feelings.

☐ 16. You have a goal of learning three new things each year — how to change the furnace filter, how to set your VCR, how to line dance. (Can you name three accomplishments from last year?)

☐ 17. You don't cry over anything that can't shed a tear for you.

☐ 18. You do not say yes to too many things and overextend yourself.

☐ 19. You freely give compliments and credit to others.

☐ 20. You never drink too much or use illegal drugs.

- ☐ 21. You work hard to keep the irritation out of your voice.

- ☐ 22. You have resolved your issues with your parents and have forgiven them for their flaws. You have moved to a give-and-take relationship with them.

- ☐ 23. You do not do anything that is against the law, even a minor infraction.

- ☐ 24. You work hard to overcome loneliness and depression. You do not passively give in to it.

- ☐ 25. You know how to enjoy life. You're as happy and fulfilled putting in a hard day's work as a hard day's play.

- ☐ 26. Your waking hours are spent mostly in the present, living each moment in a relaxed and accepting way.

- ☐ 27. You don't defend, get sarcastic or race to come up with an excuse when you are criticized. You think about the feedback and only after contemplation decide to accept or reject it.

- ☐ 28. You do an act of kindness each day — calling an aging parent, giving someone a phone message, fixing someone a snack.

- ☐ 29. You have learned not to sweat the little aggravations such as someone arriving late, a slow lane at the check-out counter, no toilet tissue in the bathroom.

- ☐ 30. You have realistic expectations. You fully understand that having expectations that are too high leads to anxiety and frustration and having expectations that are too low leads to boredom and lack of involvement in life.

- ☐ 31. You understand that each belief you hold, each decision you make, each behavior you present adds or subtracts from your dignity and worth as a human being.

☐ 32. You live by the following: ***"Hurt not the earth, neither the sea, nor the trees."***[30]

Revelations 7:3

☐ 33. You live by the Golden Rule: ***"So always treat others as you would like them to treat you."***[31]

Matthew 7:12

☐ 34. You understand, and live by, the following words: ***"Let there be peace on earth and let it begin with me."***[32]

Well, how did you do? Are you 95 percent there? Eighty-five percent mature?

For every checkmark give yourself a gold star and a pat on the back. Come on, take your hand, put it over your shoulder, and give yourself a pat. Funny how we like those pats and seldom give them to ourselves.

Now take a look at those items that in good conscience you couldn't check. Which of those items will you start working on?

Cats, and Love, and Change

Often when I give a talk, a person will stand up and say, "People don't change. You can't change a person."

My response is, "Oh, yes. People change."

Let me tell you a story about cats, and love, and change.

You see, all my life I've been a dog lover. My first recollection of having a dog is when I was about three or four years old. The dog's name was Bum. He came by his name honestly because he was always on the run. He would race out the door if you opened it, jump the backyard fence or chew right through whatever line was used to tie him. After Bum died, our family had a succession of dogs. There was Candy, and then Lady, and then Bootsie. When I was in first or second grade, a stray cat appeared at the door. It was the dead of winter,

CASE STUDY

15

> ***"I'm so damn mad I won't be around in the year 2010 to see what's going to happen."***
>
> Harold Thayer
> at age 84,
> former Chairman
> of the Board,
> Mallinckrodt
> Chemical

so my mom broke down and let the cat in. The cat managed to outstay his welcome in less than 48 hours. I still remember my mom saying, "I hate cats. They get into everything. Out with the cat." And the cat went. After I got married and had my own family, we got a dog.

Across town my parents now had two dogs, and in another part of town my sister, April, had two dogs. All the members of our family were confirmed dog lovers.

Then our daughter, Anna-Mary, started asking for a cat. Now how could a little girl who was surrounded by dog lovers want a cat?

She asked for a cat for her birthday, for Christmas, for being good. She pressed, and I resisted.

My husband was neutral, but deep down I think he also wanted a cat. He'd grown up on a farm with lots of cats.

One day my love for my daughter was so powerful that I said, "OK. We'll get a cat."

That was some years ago. Today we have two cats. When I come home at night, they're usually sitting in the entrance hall waiting for me. When I write, I often have one in my lap. I pet them. I play with them. You see, I've fallen in love with cats.

Do people change?

I've had people leave therapy and tell me they are different people, inside and out. They think differently, feel differently, behave differently. People get in control of their anger. They learn to manage their feelings and stop making critical and sarcastic comments. They learn to give compliments. They learn responsibility — doing what they say they'll do, staying within their budget, stopping the affairs. They monitor their drinking or give it up entirely. They stop procrastinating. They go back to school, change jobs, start dating. They learn to be generous. And they learn to love.

No one stays the same.

> ***"To be without some of the things you want is an indispensable part of happiness."***
>
> Anonymous

Are you the same arrogant or scared kid you were in high school? No way.

Have you learned a new sport or taken up a new hobby in the past 10 years? Of course you have.

Have you learned to use a computer, set a VCR, program your answering machine, run a fax, use a cordless telephone, use an ATM machine?

Remember *Alice in Wonderland*?
She's talking to the Caterpillar.

"Who are you?" said the Caterpillar ...
Alice replied, rather shyly, "I-I hardly know, sir, just at present — at least I know who I was when I got up this morning, but I think I must have been changed several times since then."[33]

Heading for Happiness

I've known Annie for years. When I was in college, I taught her four boys to swim.

About 10 years later, when I was a therapist, I met Annie again. This time she came to me because she and her husband, Bert, were fighting terribly over their youngest son, Kevin.

"Bert could see Kevin had a problem," she said. "I had my head in the clouds. I couldn't believe Kevin was into drugs. Finally he got in trouble with the law, robbed a house, so I had to change my tune.

"Bert and I disagreed on how to handle Kevin. We fought bitterly. Bert moved out, and I took over. It was a nightmare. Kevin would take money from my purse to support his habit. He took my jewelry and sold it for drug money. It took me several years to realize that I had to practice tough love and Kevin had to leave. Eventually Kevin cleaned up his act, but it took years.

"Bert and I were separated for nine months. Through counselling I learned to discipline and also not to get so upset when my husband was critical. He was critical, and I was passive. We got back together and lived on pretty good terms for another eight years before he died."

Two years after Bert's death, Annie was diagnosed with ovarian cancer.

"I went through chemotherapy and lost all my hair. It came back curly. That was good."

CASE STUDY

15

> ***"Just think how happy you'd be if you lost everything you have right now — and then got it back again."***
>
> Apples of Gold

Several years later Annie was diagnosed with breast cancer and had a mastectomy. She was also in bad financial shape. A mutual friend called and told me Annie was in trouble, so I called her. I said, "I've got a great therapy group that meets on Tuesday nights, and I have one spot left."

She said, "I'm poor."

I said, "So what? Do you want the spot?"

She started to laugh and cry and said, "Thank you. Thank you. I'll take it."

That was three years ago.

"My group has given me a lot of support," says Annie. "My grandson has cystic fibrosis. He just celebrated his 16th birthday. I'm so happy.

"My group has seen me through the death of my 31-year-old daughter-in-law, who died of a rare form of breast cancer. After she died, I lived with my son and five-year-old grandson for six months, trying to take care of them.

"My group supported me through several more biopsies. The doctors found cancer again, this time in my back. More chemotherapy, a staph infection that about did me in, blood clots in my legs and the loss of my curly hair.

"But now I'm just fine.

"I'm making my granddaughter jumpers for school. I'm painting the bathroom ceiling a burnt orange. I dressed four dolls for my church to give to poor families at Christmas. I have my flowers to take care of. I have six grandchildren and lots of friends.

"I tell you, every day is an experience. I think you get out of life what you put in. You can be happy, sad, angry. I elect to be happy. I program myself to be happy. I say, 'You have today, let's see what you can put into it.' I wake up and I'm happy to be here. It takes too much energy to be crabby."

Then Annie giggled. Annie is always giggling and smiling and laughing. She knows the secret of happiness.

I Bet You Know the Secret, Too

Here are a few of my own happinesses:

- Standing upright and stretching after being bent over in the garden
- Washing the dirt off my scraped and overworked hands
- Walking fast, faster and then breaking into a run
- Hearing my husband sing in the shower
- Reading a column to a friend over the telephone just after I've finished writing it
- Seeing a note from my daughter on my nightstand
- Doing my Nordic Track with Elvis blaring in the background. And then getting such a rush of energy that I jump off and dance like a maniac until I can hardly breathe
- Having my mom say, "Let me give you a backrub"
- Hearing our daughter put the key in the door before curfew
- Having the telephone ring and hearing one of our sons' voices
- Wanting to say something critical and not saying anything at all
- Laughing so hard I hurt

Now it's your turn ...

"I want to put a ding in the universe."

Steven Jobs

Ordering Additional Copies:

If you would like to order additional copies of ***BEING OK JUST ISN'T ENOUGH*** for your organization, business colleagues, friends or family, call: NATIONAL SEMINARS GROUP at 1-800-258-7248.

Got a Group to Train?

If you would like to attend a seminar on ***BEING OK JUST ISN'T ENOUGH***, call us. Participants return to work armed with new tools, practical strategies and powerful skills that enhance their effectiveness immediately. You can schedule training where and when it is most convenient for you! We can train your group on-site at your location.

Plus, as an added value, we will customize ***BEING OK JUST ISN'T ENOUGH*** to meet your organization's specific objectives. With group training from National Seminars, you'll get MORE for LESS ...

- ✓ **MORE time** left for you — When you partner with us, you save time and money on development, administration and delivery ... we do the work, you get the results — fast!
- ✓ **LESS** turnaround time from training request to delivery
- ✓ **MORE focus** on the exact needs of your organization and your people
- ✓ **LESS "generic"** information
- ✓ **MORE positive change** when many associates absorb new ideas and learn new methods at the same time
- ✓ **LESS chance** that people will miss out on learning
- ✓ **MORE value** for your training dollar — Our no-hassle curriculum licensing agreement means you can cascade the learning throughout your organization
- ✓ **LESS total investment** per associate

If you are expected to do MORE with LESS, join the thousands of organizations that choose National Seminars for customized training. Call us at 1-800-344-4613, ext. 3051, to discover how easy and cost-effective it is to partner with us. Think of us as your Corporate University.™

NOTES

All names in this book have been changed. In a few stories, minor changes have been made to protect someone's identity.

CHAPTER 1: Why Go Through Life and Not Understand Yourself?

1. Thomas F. Crum, *The Magic of Conflict* (New York: Simon & Schuster, 1987), 223-224.

2. Source unknown.

3. *Plato*, trans. by B. Jowett (New York: Walter J. Black, 1942), 56.

4. *The New Jerusalem Bible*, Ephesians 5:14 (New York: Doubleday & Company, Inc., 1985), 1937.

CHAPTER 2: Are You an Outer-Focused or Inner-Focused Person?

5. Anthony de Mello, *The Song Of The Bird* (New York: Doubleday & Company, Inc., 1982), 8.

CHAPTER 3: Are You Aware of Your Psychological Boundary Lines?

6. William Shakespeare, *Hamlet* ed. by Susanne L. Wofford (New York: Bedford Books of St. Martin's Press, 1994), 2, 2, 245, 68.

CHAPTER 4: Do You Know and Practice the Eight Principles of Love?

7. Characters from the comic strip, *Mother Goose and Grimm* by Gibson Greetings, Inc. Cincinnati, 1992.

8. Merle Shain, *Hearts That We Broke Long Ago* (New York: Bantam Books, 1983), 71.

CHAPTER 5: Do You Get Too Angry?

9. Carol Tavris, *ANGER: The Misunderstood Emotion* (New York: Simon & Schuster, 1989), 83.

10. Solomon Schimmel, *The Seven Deadly Sins* (New York: The Free Press, 1992), 91, citing St. Thomas Aquinas, *Summa Theologica* Volume 44, 2a2ae (New York: McGraw Hill, 1964), 120-121.

CHAPTER 6: How Do You Handle Suffering and Disappointment?

11. Charles S. Prebish, *The Historical Dictionary of Buddhism* (Metuchen, NJ: Scarecrow Press, 1993), 54.

CHAPTER 7: Are You Aware of How the Werther Effect and the Consistency Principle Influence Your Everyday Life?

12. William T. Hornaday, "The Extermination of the American Bison," *Report of National Museum*, 1887, 421.

13. Kurt Kauter, "A Tale for all Seasons," New Fables: "Thus Spoke The Caribou," in Thomas F. Crum, *The Magic of Conflict* (New York: Simon & Schuster, 1987), 250.

CHAPTER 9: Are You a Faultfinding, Critical Person?

14. *The New Jerusalem Bible*, Luke 6:41 (New York: Doubleday & Company, Inc., 1985), 1698.

15. Benjamin Franklin, *Benjamin Franklin's Wit and Wisdom* (Mt. Vernon, NY: Peter Pauper Press, Inc. 1960), 21.

CHAPTER 10: How Jealous and Competitive Are You?

16. Moshe C. Luzzatto, *The Path of the Just*, trans. by Shraga Silverstein (New York: Feldheim Publishers, 1966), 165.

CHAPTER 12: Is Your Thinking Positive or Negative? Past, Present, or Future Focused?

17. Oliver Sacks, *The Man Who Mistook His Wife for a Hat and Other Clinical Tales* (New York: Harper & Row, Publishers, Inc., 1987), 27.

18. Ibid., 29.

19. David K. Reynolds, *Water Bears No Scars* (New York: William Morrow and Company, Inc., 1987), 53.

20. Ken Keyes, Jr., *Handbook to Higher Consciousness*, 5th ed. (Berkeley, CA: Living Love Center, 1975), 26.

21. Ibid., 52.

22. Reynolds, 52.

23. Ram Dass and Paul Gorman, *How Can I Help?* (New York: Alfred A. Knopf, Inc., 1985), 101.

CHAPTER 14: Do You Talk to God?

24. *The New Scofield Reference Bible*, Matthew 21:22 (New York: Oxford University Press, Inc., 1967), 1028.

25. Kenneth L. Woodward, "Talking To God," *Newsweek*, 6 January 1992, 40.

26. "Why We Pray," *Life*, 17 March 1994, 54-62.

27. Rabbi Rona Shapiro, "Prayer," Sermon preached on Yom Kippur 5755, on 15 September, 1994, Berkeley Hillel, Berkeley, CA. Story paraphrased from David J. Wolpe, *Teaching Your Children About God, A Modern Jewish Approach* (New York: HarperCollins Publishers, Inc., 1993), 44.

28. *Tanakh, The Holy Scriptures*, Deuteronomy 6:4 (New York: The Jewish Publication Society, 1988), 284.

29. *The New Jerusalem Bible*, Psalm 23 (New York: Doubleday & Company, Inc., 1985), 611.

CHAPTER 15: Living in a State of Maturity, Contentment and Happiness

30. *The New Scofield Reference Bible*, Revelations 7:3 (New York: Oxford University Press, Inc., 1967), 1358.

31. *The New Jerusalem Bible*, Matthew 7:12 (New York: Doubleday & Company, Inc., 1985), 1620.

32. Sy Miller and Jill Jackson, *"Let There Be Peace On Earth"* (Honokaa, HI: Jan-Lee Music, 1955 and 1983).

33. Lewis Carroll, *Alice in Wonderland* (New York: Grosset & Dunlap, Publishers, 1994), 43-44.

BIBLIOGRAPHY

Apples of Gold. Compiled by Jo Petty. Norwalk, CT: C. R. Gibson Company, 1962.

Averill, James R. *Anger and Aggression: An Essay on Emotion*. New York: Springer-Verlag, 1982.

Berkowitz, Leonard. "The Case for Bottling Up Rage." *Psychology Today* 7 (July 1973): 24.

Blanchard, Kenneth, and Norman Vincent Peale. *The Power of Ethical Management*. New York: Fawcett Crest, 1988.

Brand, Paul, and Philip Yancey. "And God Created Pain." *Christianity Today* 10 (January 1994): 18-23.

Burns, David D. *Feeling Good: The New Mood Therapy*. New York: William Morrow & Company, Inc., 1980.

Buss, Arnold H., and Robert A. Plomin. *A Temperament Theory of Personality Development*. London: John Wiley & Sons, 1975.

Canfield, Jack, and Mark Victor Hansen. *Chicken Soup for the Soul*. Deerfield Beach, FL: Health Communications, Inc., 1993.

Carroll, Lewis. *Alice in Wonderland*. New York: Grosset & Dunlap, Inc., 1994.

Characters from the comic strip, *Mother Goose and Grimm*. Cincinnati, OH: Gibson Greetings, Inc., 1992.

Chapman, Robert L., ed. *Roget A to Z*. New York: Harper-Collins Publishers, 1994.

Cialdini, Robert B. *Influence: Science & Practice*. New York: Harper & Row, 1988.

Copp, Jay. "What Are You Praying For?" *U.S. Catholic* 57 (July 1992): 34-38.

Crum, Thomas F. *The Magic of Conflict*. New York: Simon & Schuster, 1987.

Cunningham, Lawrence S. "Why People Still Put Their Body and Soul into Prayer." *U.S. Catholic* 58 (July 1993): 6-13.

Dass, Ram, and Paul Gorman. *How Can I Help?* New York: Alfred A. Knopf, Inc., 1985.

Dossey, Larry. *Healing Words: The Power of Prayer and the Practice of Medicine*. San Francisco: HarperCollins Publishers, Inc., 1993.

Dulbecco, Renato, ed. *Encyclopedia of Human Biology*. New York: Academic Press, Inc., 1991. s.v. "Thinking," by K. J. Gilhooly

Eardley, Linda. "Drinking Students Suspended." *St. Louis Post Dispatch*, 27 April 1994, B-1.

Editors of Conari Press. *Random Acts of Kindness*. Berkeley, CA: Conari Press, 1993.

Evatt, Chris, and Bruce Feld. *The Givers and the Takers*. New York: Ballantine Books, 1983.

Franklin, Benjamin. *Benjamin Franklin's Wit and Wisdom*. Mt. Vernon, NY: Peter Pauper Press, Inc., 1960.

Fry, Christopher. *A Sleep of Prisoners*. New York: Oxford University Press, 1951.

God's Little Instruction Book. Tulsa, OK: Honor Books, Inc., 1993.

Goethe, Johann Wolfgang von. *The Sorrows of Young Werther*. New York: Penguin Books USA, Inc., 1962.

Goldman, Ari L. "Religion Notes." *New York Times*, 9 April 1994: A-10.

Haley, Alyssa. *Your 30-Day Journey to Kicking the Procrastination Habit.* Nashville, TN: Thomas Nelson Publishers, 1992.

Halpern, Howard M. *How to Break Your Addiction to a Person.* New York: Bantam Books, 1982.

Harris, P. L. "Infant Cognition." In *Handbook of Child Psychology*, ed. Paul H. Mussen. 4th ed. Volume 2. *Infancy and Developmental Psychobiology*. New York: John Wiley & Sons, 1983.

Helmering, Doris Wild. *Happily Ever After*. New York: Warner Books, Inc., 1986.

——. "At Last a Fancy for Felines." *St. Louis Post-Dispatch,* 4 April 1992.

——. "Controlling Behavior Can Be Active or Passive." *St. Louis Post-Dispatch*, 29 May 1991.

——. "Dad, Do You Remember When?" *St. Louis Post-Dispatch*, 15 June 1988.

——. "Differing Standards Are a Cause for Conflict." *St. Louis Post-Dispatch*, 12 July 1993.

—— "Don't Assume You Are Center of the Universe." *St. Louis Post-Dispatch*, 3 January 1994.

——. "Focus on the Past Reflects Changing Life." *St. Louis Post Dispatch*, 8 November 1989.

——. "Foot-in-Mouth Types Often Trample on Others." *St. Louis Post-Dispatch*, 17 February 1988.

——. "Give Others Sunshine, Not Dreary Rain Shower." *St. Louis Post-Dispatch*, 28 March 1994.

——. "Maybe Might Be Best Answer of All." *St. Louis Post-Dispatch*, 11 July 1992.

——. "Memories of Mom on Her Birthday." *St. Louis Post-Dispatch*, 23 October 1995.

——. "Secret Spending Costs $35,000 in Savings." *St. Louis Post-Dispatch*, 2 May 1990.

——. "Tiff over Flowers Is Really about Control." *St. Louis Post-Dispatch*, 7 June 1989.

——. "Unkind Responses Fatal to Intimacy." *St. Louis Post-Dispatch*, 9 November 1991.

———. "When It's Time to Hang up the Keys." *St. Louis Post-Dispatch*, 7 March 1994.

Hokanson, Jack E. "Psychophysiological Evaluation of the Catharsis Hypothesis." In *The Dynamics of Aggression*, ed. by E.I. Megargee and J.E. Hokanson. New York: Harper & Row, Publishers, Inc., 1970.

Hokanson, Jack E., and Michael Burgess. "The Effects of Status, Type of Frustration and Aggression on Vascular Processes." *Journal of Abnormal and Social Psychology* 65 (1962): 232-237.

Hornaday, William T. "The Extermination of the American Bison." *Report of National Museum*, 1887.

Houston, Jean. *The Possible Human.* New York: St. Martin's Press, 1982.

International Thesaurus of Quotations. Compiled by Rhoda Thomas Tripp. New York: Thomas Y. Crowell Company, 1970.

James, Jennifer. *Success Is the Quality of Your Journey*. Seattle: Jennifer James, Inc., 1983.

Jung, C. G. *Psychological Types*. Princeton, NJ: Princeton University Press, 1971.

Keyes, Jr., Ken. *Handbook to Higher Consciousness*. 5th ed. Berkeley, CA: Living Love Center, 1975.

Kushner, Harold. *When Bad Things Happen to Good People.* New York: Schocken Books, 1981.

———. *Who Needs God*. New York: Simon & Schuster Inc., 1989.

Luzzatto, Moshe C. *The Path of the Just,* Trans. by Shraga Silverstein. New York: Feldheim Publishers, 1966.

Martin, Julia Vituello-Martin and J. Robert Moskin. *The Executive's Book of Quotations*. New York: Oxford University Press, 1994.

Mayer, Richard. *Thinking, Problem Solving, Cognition*. New York: W. H. Freeman and Company, 1983.

McGinnis, Alan Loy. *Bringing Out the Best in People*. Minneapolis: Augsburg Publishing House, 1985.

McWilliams, John-Rogers and Peter McWilliams. *Do It! Let's Get off Our Butts*. Los Angeles: Prelude Press, Inc., 1991.

Mello, Anthony de. *The Song of the Bird.* New York: Doubleday and Company, Inc., 1982.

Miller, Sy, and Jill Jackson. "*Let There Be Peace on Earth.*" Honokaa, HI: Jan-Lee Music, 1955 and 1983.

Murdock, Mike. *The Double Diamond Principle*. Dallas, TX: Wisdom International, Inc. for Mike Murdock Evangelistic Association, 1990.

Mussen, Paul; John Conger; Jerome Kagan; and Aletha Huston. *Child Development And Personality*. New York: Harper & Row, Publishers, Inc., 1990.

Muto, Susan. "The Threefold Path to Peaceful Intimacy." *Liguorian* 82 (January 1994): 18-24.

Paulhus, L. Delroy. "Bypassing the Will: The Automatization of Affirmations." In *Handbook Of Mental Control*, ed. by Daniel M. Wegner and James W. Pennebaker, 573-578. Englewood Cliffs, NJ: Prentice-Hall, Inc., 1993.

Peck, M. Scott. *The Road Less Traveled.* New York: Simon and Schuster, 1978.

Plato. trans. by B. Jowett. New York: Walter J. Black, 1942.

Prebish, Charles S. *The Historical Dictionary of Buddhism*. Metuchen, NJ: Scarecrow Press, 1993.

Ramachandran, V. S., ed. *Encyclopedia of Human Behavior*. New York: Academic Press, 1994. s.v. "Extraversion - Introversion," by D. H. Saklofshe and H. J. Eysenck and "Individual Differences in Temperament," by Louis A. Schmidt, Ariana Shahinfar, and Nathan A. Fox.

Reisman, David. *The Lonely Crowd*. New Haven, CT: Yale University Press, 1950.

Reps, Paul. *Zen Flesh, Zen Bones.* Rutland, VT: Charles E. Tuttle Company, Inc., 1957.

Reynolds, David K. *Water Bears No Scars*. New York: William Morrow and Company, Inc., 1987.

Ripple, Paula. *Growing Strong at Broken Places*. Notre Dame, IN: Ave Maria Press, 1986.

Sacks, Oliver. *The Man Who Mistook His Wife for a Hat and Other Clinical Tales.* New York: Harper & Row, Publishers, Inc., 1987.

Sadker, Myra, and David Sadker. *Failing at Fairness*. New York: Charles Scribner's Sons, 1994.

Salovey, Peter; Christopher K. Hsee; and John D. Mayer, "Emotional Intelligence and the Self-Regulation of Affect." In *Handbook Of Mental Control*, ed. by Daniel M. Wegner and James W. Pennebaker, 258-277. Englewood Cliffs, NJ: Prentice-Hall, Inc., 1993.

Schiff, Jacqui Lee. *Cathexis Reader*. New York: Harper & Row, Publishers, Inc., 1975.

Schimmel, Solomon. *The Seven Deadly Sins.* New York: The Free Press, 1992.

Shain, Merle. *Hearts That We Broke Long Ago*. New York: Bantam Books, 1983.

Shakespeare, William. *Hamlet*, ed. by Susanne L. Wofford. New York: Bedford Books of St. Martin's Press, 1994.

Shapiro, Rabbi Rona, "Prayer." Sermon preached on Yom Kippur 5755, on 15 September, 1994, Berkeley Hillel, Berkeley, CA. Story paraphrased from David J. Wolpe, *Teaching Your Children About God, A Modern Jewish Approach*. New York: HarperCollins Publishers, Inc., 1993.

Spezzano, Charles. "What to Do Between Birth and Death." *Psychology Today* 25 (January/February 1992): 543-55+

Spielberger, Charles; Susan Krasner; and Eldra Solomon. "The Experience, Expression and Control of Anger." In *Individual Differences, Stress, and Health Psychology*, ed. by M.P. Janisse. New York: Springer-Verlag, 1988.

Tanakh, The Holy Scriptures. New York: The Jewish Publication Society, 1988.

Tavris, Carol. *ANGER, The Misunderstood Emotion*. Rev. ed. New York: Simon & Schuster, 1989.

The Wellesley College Center for Research on Women. *The AAUW Report: How Schools Shortchange Girls*. Washington, DC: American Association of University Women Education Foundation, 1992.

The New Jerusalem Bible. New York: Doubleday & Company Inc., 1985.

The New Scofield Reference Bible. New York: Oxford University Press, Inc., 1967.

Tice, Dianne M, and Roy F. Baumeister. "Controlling Anger: Self-Induced Emotion Change." In *Handbook Of Mental Control*, ed. by Daniel M. Wegner and James W. Pennebaker, 393-409. Englewood Cliffs, NJ: Prentice-Hall, Inc., 1993.

Thomas, John B. "How to Be Happier." *St. Louis Post-Dispatch*, 22 August 1993.

Volland, Victor. "More Students Suspended for Drinking." *St. Louis Post-Dispatch*, 1 May 1994, D-1.

Weiss, Robert S. "Loneliness." *The Harvard Medical School Mental Health Letter* 4 (June 1988): 4-6.

"Why We Pray." *Life* 17 (March 1994): 54-60+

Wilkins, Rich. *Going Beyond a Positive Mental Attitude*. Shepherdsville, KY: POS Publications, 1993.

Wolpe, David J. *Teaching Your Children About God*. New York: HarperCollins Publishers, Inc., 1993.

Woodward, Kenneth L. "Talking to God." *Newsweek*, (6 January 1992): 38.

Zillmann, Dolf. "Mental Control of Angry Aggression." In *Handbook Of Mental Control*, ed. by Daniel M. Wegner and James W. Pennebaker, 370-392. Englewood Cliffs, NJ: Prentice-Hall, Inc., 1993.

INDEX

YOUR BACK-OF-THE-BOOK STORE

ORDER FORM

Because you already know the value of National Press Publications Desktop Handbooks and Business User's Manuals, here's a time-saving way to purchase more career-building resources from our convenient "bookstore."

- IT'S EASY … Just make your selections, then visit us on the Web, mail, call or fax your order. (See back for details.)
- INCREASE YOUR EFFECTIVENESS … Books in these two series have sold more than two million copies and are known as reliable sources of instantly helpful information.
- THEY'RE CONVENIENT TO USE … Each handbook is durable, concise and filled with quality advice that will last you all the way to the boardroom.
- YOUR SATISFACTION IS 100% GUARANTEED. Forever.

60-MINUTE TRAINING SERIES™ HANDBOOKS

TITLE	RETAIL PRICE*	QTY.	TOTAL
8 Steps for Highly Effective Negotiations #424	$14.95		
Assertiveness #4422	$14.95		
Balancing Career and Family #4152	$14.95		
Common Ground #4122	$14.95		
The Essentials of Business Writing #4310	$14.95		
Everyday Parenting Solutions #4862	$14.95		
Exceptional Customer Service #4882	$14.95		
Fear & Anger: Control Your Emotions #4302	$14.95		
Fundamentals of Planning #4301	$14.95		
Getting Things Done #4112	$14.95		
How to Coach an Effective Team #4308	$14.95		
How to De-Junk Your Life #4306	$14.95		
How to Handle Conflict and Confrontation #4952	$14.95		
How to Manage Your Boss #493	$14.95		
How to Supervise People #4102	$14.95		
How to Work With People #4032	$14.95		
Inspire and Motivate: Performance Reviews #4232	$14.95		
Listen Up: Hear What's Really Being Said #4172	$14.95		
Motivation and Goal-Setting #4962	$14.95		
A New Attitude #4432	$14.95		
The New Dynamic Comm. Skills for Women #4309	$14.95		
The Polished Professional #4262	$14.95		
The Power of Innovative Thinking #428	$14.95		
The Power of Self-Managed Teams #4222	$14.95		
Powerful Communication Skills #4132	$14.95		
Present With Confidence #4612	$14.95		
The Secret to Developing Peak Performers #4962	$14.95		
Self-Esteem: The Power to Be Your Best #4642	$14.95		
Shortcuts to Organized Files and Records #4307	$14.95		
The Stress Management Handbook #4842	$14.95		
Supreme Teams: How to Make Teams Work #4303	$14.95		
Thriving on Change #4212	$14.95		
Women and Leadership #4632	$14.95		